COME, WALK WITH ME

Come, Walk With Me

A spiritual adventure gathering jewels

Joy Sands

PYXIS PUBLICATIONS

Copyright © 2015 Come, Walk With Me   Joy Sands
All rights reserved.
No part of this publication may be reproduced or transmitted in any form or by any means, electronic or mechanical, including photocopy, recording or any information storage and retrieval system, without permission in writing from the publisher.
Published by Pyxis Publications
Corsham SN13 8JN
Cover Design by BespokeBookCovers
Printed by CPI in the United Kingdom

Unless otherwise stated all Scripture quotations are taken from;
New International Version (NIV)
Copyright ©1973, 1978, 1984, by the International Bible Society
Anglicisation ©1979, 1986 by Hodder and Stoughton Limited

Other versions used are:

New Living Translation (NLT)
Scripture quotations are taken from the *Holy Bible,* New Living Translation, copyright ©
Used by permission of Tyndale House Publishers, Inc.,
All rights reserved.

The Message (MSG)
"Scripture taken from THE MESSAGE Copyright ©
1993,1994,1995,1996,2000,2001,2002 Used by permission of NavPress Publishing Group"

New King James Version (NKJV)
Scripture taken from the New King James Version
Copyright © 1982 by Thomas Nelson, Inc. Used by permission
All rights reserved.

ISBN 978-0-9935112-0-2

Acknowledgements

I should like to begin by thanking the following for all their help and encouragement in the writing and production of this book.
First of all to my friends, (you know who you are, my love and blessings to you all) and also my family. You don't know how much your words have encouraged and helped me.

My editor Sarah Stockinger is and has been invaluable in these final days of editing and publishing - may she be richly blessed.

I would also like to thank David Johnson for all his most valued help regarding computer 'technicalities'.

My thanks to my friend and fellow author Ruth Johnson, who with her husband Brian has helped me tremendously.

Last but definitely not least, my thanks to Basil, my ever patient and supportive husband. He is a true Ephesians 5 v28 husband.

And finally,
'It is good to give thanks to the Lord
And to sing praises to your name, O Most High,' Psalm 92:1

Further copies of Come, Walk With Me can be obtained from:

Pyxis Publications
Corsham, SN13 8JN
£8.99

CONTENTS		PAGE
Introduction		
How It All Began		1
Day 1	Grace	3
Day 2	Truth	23
Day 3	The Blood of Christ	41
Day 4	The Kingdom	59
Day 5	Glory	87
Day 6	Peace	103
Day 7	Victory	117
Day 8	Faith	135
Day 9	Salvation	153
Day 10	Praise	171
Day 11	Love	185
Day 12	Obedience	201
Day 13	Righteousness	213
Day 14	Death	227
Day 15	Treasure	241
Day 16	Crowns	245
	Post Script	255

INTRODUCTION

IT ALL HAPPENED one February. I had previously been introduced to 'The Father's House – a way of Prayer,' at a Christian day seminar, and it was this special day that launched me into meeting with the Lord in a more wonderful way.

We were invited to visit the 'Father's House' and whichever room we chose to enter would designate a special topic of prayer. For instance going into the Study meant looking into the Word of God and allowing the reading to lead into prayer. If we chose the Garden, which was included, we would spend time thinking of His wonderful creation, and thanking and praising him for it. Other rooms would lead into intimacy with the Lord, spiritual warfare, intercession, or feasting in His presence. If we needed to spend time in repentance then the Bathroom was the place to go, forgiveness would follow and spiritual cleansing take place. So as a group, we all went before the Lord and prayed according to the various rooms that we chose, sharing our experiences afterwards. We expected to be led initially to a room where we felt at home and for me this meant the Study. We could move on to other rooms at the Holy Spirit's leading.

There was one small room called the Closet. Jesus spoke about the closet when He was teaching the people about prayer. He had noticed that when the Pharisees and other leaders wanted to pray, they chose to do so in the streets where everyone could observe them and be impressed by their fine speaking and religious attitude. Jesus was not impressed. He taught the people to go into the closet (a small private room) when they wanted to pray and spend time with God. He would see what was done in secret and reward them.

We do not tend to use the word 'closet' in the UK these days, but in times past, it was a well -known room leading from the main bedroom and used as a quiet and private space. Now we tend to use the study, the office or the bedroom to find that quiet and personal place. John and Charles Wesley's mother had no such luxury. When she wanted some space to pray, she would sit and cover her face with her apron and her large family then understood that on no account were they to interrupt her!

However, I was somewhat intrigued by the Closet as it held the possibility of receiving visions from the Lord. It was this small room that began to grip my attention. Visions! Would I, and could I?

The next day I decided to use 'The Fathers House' way of prayer. I chose to go to the Study first and then perhaps to the Closet. In the event, these two 'rooms' with their topics of prayer were used exclusively and I was glad of the advice to keep a journal. This has enabled my prayer conversations with the Lord to be included here verbatim. When the visions faded, I went to the Study where the Bible, (my plumb-line of God's truth) would teach me further. These Bible sections are recorded as a series of cameos or tasters, as each topic (or jewel) warrants a full book. Thus in this month of February, I used 'The Father's House' to guide my prayer time with God. So come - let me share my journal with you.

HOW IT ALL BEGAN

'Whenever we come into God's presence, He requires that we bring Him various gifts or sacrifices. These spiritual gifts are thanksgiving, praise and worship.'

Derek Prince

As always I begin my time with the Lord in praise and worship. Then prayerfully going to the Study for the Word, I read this: 'The kingdom of heaven is like treasure hidden in a field. When a man found it, he hid it again, and then in his joy went and sold all he had and bought that field.'[1]

Treasure! The word impacted me. 'Treasure' for me meant an encounter with the Lord, and to sell all meant to put everything aside; all interruptions and all distractions and to take time to seek Him. My inclination then was to praise Him as songs of Scripture flooded my spirit.

Then the Lord spoke:

'My dear Child,
As you take time to draw near to Me, to sit in My Presence and to bring your heart to My heart, then you will begin to know and to recognise My voice speaking to you. My Holy Spirit will make Me known to you. Be still. Lay down your cares and concerns. Trust Me, the everlasting and faithful God who loves you, Your Eternal Father who cares for you. My child, hear My still small voice.'

My thoughts now turned to approaching the Closet for prayer. As I did so, to my amazement, I realised that I was on a

---

[1] Matthew 13:44

raft in the middle of a vast sea, bobbing along on the waves. There was no land in sight nor ships, just open sea in every direction. I was alone on the raft, yet I was aware that the Lord was with me. It was the start of my experiencing visions. I began to speak to Him,

'Am I safe on this raft Lord?'

'Yes. You are safe My child. Whilst you are with Me, you are always safe. And I am always with you.'

'Where are we going Lord?'

'We are gently going into My plans and purposes. There is no current or tide under you on this raft, but My hand will push and guide the raft to where I want it to go.'

'Yes Lord. I will go wherever you want to take me.'

'This is the start of a new way for you My child.'

'But what if there is a storm?'

(Then came what sounded like a smiling rebuke.)

'Have you not heard that I still the storm?'

'Lord, I know I am on a raft but this is feeling very much like walking on water! Even so, I will go wherever you want to take me.'

'Yes child. Be patient. We are going on a journey, a new journey, learning more of Me and being in My Presence. This is an encounter, a new way, a living way. Rest in Me. I AM your peace, your direction, and your safety.'

With that, the vision faded and I was left with a variety of tumbling thoughts.

A series of special mornings followed. I always started with a time of praise and worship and by choosing to enter the Closet, was led straight into times of vision. I then went to the Study, where I could test everything by the Word of God.

DAY 1

GRACE

'Thanksgiving and praise. There is no other way into the presence of God.'   *Derek Prince*
'Grace is the voice that calls us to change and gives us the power to pull it off.'   *Max Lucado*
'My grace is sufficient for you, for my power is made perfect in weakness.'[2]   *2 Corinthians 12:9*

A NEW MORNING and I awake in anticipation. Would I be on the raft again? Reading Psalm 100 led me back into worship, then just as suddenly as before I found I was not on the raft, but this time walking on a Beach.

It was delightful. A large sand and pebble Beach, blue sea on my left, with gentle rolling waves coming to the shore. The air warm, the sky also blue and there was a feeling of sheer delight to be walking along at the water's edge, knowing that the Lord was with me. Then I became aware that He wanted me to look for treasure, and I knew that He would tell me more about it and help me to find it. Somewhere amongst the pebbles would be what He wanted me to find and it would hold a special

---

[2] 2 Corinthians 12:9

significance. It would be treasure of some sort, but what? So on this, the first of what was to be many such walks, I kept walking and looking. Just ahead of me I saw something amongst the pebbles. There was no mistaking it. Before my eyes was the most exquisite black jewel. It radiated light. It had depths in its blackness that brought colour to mind, yet there were no colours to be seen, just an amazing rich blackness. It was the most beautiful and intriguing black jewel I had ever seen - so very lovely.

As I looked I heard Him say; '**This is your first jewel. Overcome and there will be no disappointment. Know the discipline of being still. Let all anxieties go. We have plenty of time, precious time, together.**'

I was able to ask,

'What is the meaning of this stone Lord?'

'**It is the beauty of My grace. My grace is sufficient for you.**'

But why would the grace jewel be black? Black is so often associated with death or sin. It seemed strange to me, so I asked the Lord about it and He replied;

'**Black is the presence of all the colours and in the same way My grace encompasses all your needs. It is totally sufficient for you at all times and in all situations. Experience My grace in gloriously happy times, in sad times, in troubled times, even in difficult conversations. My grace is all you need.**'

So I picked up this lovely stone of grace and held it. My thoughts vacillated between being overwhelmed by its beauty and thinking about God's grace. Standing there, enjoying the scene before me, and watching the waves come gently in, I thought about our conversation. Then I wanted to look into God's Word, and the vision faded.

Grace

HOW MAY WE DESCRIBE GOD'S GRACE? It is the outpouring of His special love upon us in every way possible and in every way needed. This special grace is that which comes from Jesus Christ and is available to the one who has put his or her trust in Him. The Scripture says that grace and truth came through Jesus Christ.[3] It is true that the Lord pours blessing on believers and non-believers alike, for as Jesus said; 'He causes His sun to rise on the evil and the good, and sends rain on the righteous and the unrighteous.'[4] Yet this special grace of God that comes from Christ is a wonder, resulting from His sacrificial death and is available to His people. The epitome of God's grace is found here,

'In Him we have redemption through His blood, the forgiveness of sins, in accordance with the riches of God's grace that He lavished on us with all wisdom and understanding.'[5] The pinnacle of His grace to us is found when we experience our total forgiveness, knowing that we are redeemed and eternal salvation is ours.

In the UK we understand about 'Grace and Favour Homes', manors and mansions belonging to the Queen that friends and family may use freely at her invitation. In the same

---

[3] John 1:17
[4] Matthew 5:45
[5] Ephesians 1:7-8

way, we too as children of God may receive grace and favour from the Lord, as we believe and trust in Christ. Is it free for us? Yes, because the price has already been paid by Jesus Christ; it is the Gospel or Good News that introduces us to this amazing grace. The Apostle Peter wrote, 'For you know that God paid a ransom to save you from the empty life you inherited from your ancestors. And the ransom he paid was not mere gold or silver. He paid for you with the precious lifeblood of Christ, the sinless, spotless Lamb of God.'[6]

There is a little acronym that is used to help us understand grace which we will explore:

GOD'S **R**ICHES **A**T **C**HRIST'S EXPENSE

GOD'S **R**ICHES are limitless. He who created galaxies, universes, mankind and all that is, gently reminded the prophet Isaiah of His greatness,

'This is what the Lord says:
"Heaven is my throne,
and the earth is my footstool.[7]
Where is the house you will build for me?
Where will my resting place be?
Has not my hand made all these things,
and so they came into being?" declares the Lord.' [8]

---

[6] 1Peter 1:18-19 NLT
[7] Also spoken by Jesus - Matthew:5:34-35a
[8] Isaiah 66:1

Yet amazingly we get the impression from the Apostle Paul when he is writing to the Ephesian Church, that God Himself, who has no need of anything, has a special inheritance which delights Him. This inheritance is to Him rich and glorious.[9] Our God, who is so rich in all ways possible, calls us, the redeemed ones, His glorious inheritance. We are His treasure. The New Living Translation adds this alternative translation in a footnote to this same verse,
'I want you to realise how much God has been honoured by acquiring his people'.[10]

If we but realised the depth of His love for us, we would surely spend more time in His presence. He is not only the God of unsearchable riches, but is the One who delights in bestowing many of them upon those He calls His own. Paul verbalises the enormity of this concept when writing about the Lord to the believers in Rome,

'Oh, the depth of the riches of the wisdom and knowledge of God! How unsearchable his judgments, and his paths beyond tracing out!'[11]

Paul, again writing to the Roman church, urges them not to show contempt or despise the special riches that are part of God's character and His very being. These are the riches of His goodness, of His immense patience and forbearance, and His long-suffering. How easy it is for us too, to take His patience for granted, not realising that God is looking for us to

---

[9] Ephesians 1:18
[10] Ephesians 1:18 NLT
[11] Romans 11:33

come to repentance over certain issues.[12] So we can understand that the riches of God are not only earthly riches but they also contain the unmistakable riches found in His character, His attributes, and His immense love toward us. The grace of God poured out to us is indeed full of the riches of God and comes to us at Christ's most costly expense.

We don't have to be wealthy or clever, influential or important, popular or attractive, talented or creative, loved or appreciated, good or religious in order to experience God's grace. None of these things, wonderful as they may be, count with God. He just looks for the one who believes in Jesus Christ, who turns from his sin in repentance and with the help of the Holy Spirit, chooses to walk in obedience to Him. It means acknowledging His Lordship.
Jesus said this;
'Are you tired? Worn out? Burned out on religion? Come to me. Get away with me and you'll recover your life. I'll show you how to take a real rest. Walk with Me and work with me - watch how I do it. Learn the unforced rhythms of grace. I won't lay anything heavy or ill-fitting on you. Keep company with me and you'll learn to live freely and lightly.'[13]

The most wonderful thing about His grace is once we have taken this step, we can call upon the Lord at all times, in all places, and for all reasons. We can also enjoy times of worshipping Him that bring a deep spiritual delight. We discover that the Holy Spirit provides spiritual gifts which help

---

[12] Romans 2:4
[13] Matthew 11:28-30 MSG

us throughout our lives, also enabling us to help others. Some would say, 'We are blessed to be a blessing.'

There are also many times when we have a particular need and without even asking, the Lord pours out His grace upon us and brings relief.[14] Having entered into relationship with Jesus Christ (which is an amazing reality in itself), we begin to understand more and more about His love for us. Just as a rose is beautiful and gives out perfume, so Jesus Christ is a delight to us. His grace is like a sweet perfume, which when poured out causes us to be both a sweet aroma to God and to others. Paul expounds it like this;
'But thanks be to God, who always leads us in triumphal procession in Christ and through us spreads everywhere the fragrance of the knowledge of him. For we are to God the aroma of Christ among those who are being saved and those who are perishing. To the one we are the smell of death; to the other, the fragrance of life. And who is equal to such a task?'[15]

This truth is often revealed when we share the love of Christ with others. The Christ in us will either draw them to Him or offend and repel them. Yet the nature of grace is that it is free. We can't earn it and we don't deserve it. Paul the Apostle says that it's through our faith in Christ and by His grace that we are saved;
'For it is by grace you have been saved, through faith - and this not from yourselves, it is the gift of God - not by works, so that

---

[14] Matthew 6:8 NLT
[15] 2 Corinthians 2:14-16

no one may boast.'[16]

It is evident that we can't do a single thing to save ourselves. No amount of good deeds, giving money or time, even attending Church services and going through religious rituals will qualify us for salvation, which contains the promise of eternal life with God. How many people do we know who think that by living 'good' lives, they will earn a place in heaven after death? They would have to be sinless to qualify. God offers to us a special relationship with Him and we enter in when we realise that Jesus died for our sins and in faith we repent, receiving His forgiveness. Then our new life begins.

Time and again Jesus asked people if they believed and if they had faith in Him. It was a particularly important question for those who sought healing. There was a certain synagogue ruler, Jairus, who asked Jesus to come and heal his dying daughter. Thus far Jairus believed and had faith in Jesus. But as they neared his house, news came that his daughter had died, and he was advised not to bother Jesus any more. Jesus ignored these messengers and impressed upon Jairus not to be afraid, but just to believe.[17] So they entered the house and the outcome was that the little twelve year old girl was brought back to life. Doesn't Jesus ask this of us too, "Don't be afraid, just believe?"

By the inspiration of the Holy Spirit, the Apostle Paul said that God desires all men to be saved and to come to a

---

[16] Ephesians 2:8-9
[17] Mark 5:36

knowledge of the truth.[18] He too knew that 'good works' were not the key to receiving salvation. No one had been more 'religious' and full of 'good works' than Saul, as he was called then. But when the Lord met him on the road to Damascus, all of this fell away. He then knew that there was nothing that he could 'do.' All had been done by Christ on the cross. In later years he said this,
'God saved you by his special favour when you believed. And you can't take credit for this; it is a gift from God. Salvation is not a reward for the good things we have done, so none of us can boast about it.'[19]

Apparently one of the most popular songs now at funerals is Frank Sinatra's 'I Did It My Way.' However, according to Scripture it has to be God's way. Jesus said that He Himself is the only Way that anyone can come to the Father.[20]

ETERNAL LIFE

How do we imagine eternal life? We may have many ideas of our own but Jesus said this, 'Now this is eternal life: that they may know you, the only true God, and Jesus Christ, whom You have sent.'[21] So we understand that the essence of eternal life is relationship, and knowing God. Christ has made this possible. This is what makes Christianity unique.

How do we enter eternal life? Eternal life begins in a

---

[18] 1Timothy 2:4
[19] Ephesians 2:8-9 NLT
[20] John 14:6
[21] John 17:3

similar way to physical life, which is through birth. Jesus explained this new birth, or being born again to Nicodemus, a Pharisee and a leading member of the Sanhedrin, the Jewish ruling council. He explained that in order to see the Kingdom of God a spiritual birth was needed. [22] It is this new spiritual birth that ushers us into a living relationship with God. Our new life in the Kingdom begins.

AMAZING GRACE

Everything connected with our salvation is given through the grace of God. We are saved by grace through faith. We then discover that it is by His grace we can freely approach Him in prayer as a new person, sinless and righteous. But how can we appear sinless? The Bible calls it justification and it means in simple terms, 'just-as-if-we-never-sinned.'

The Apostle Paul when preaching the Gospel to a group of Jews and God-fearing Gentiles said this by the inspiration of the Holy Spirit, 'Therefore, My brothers, I want you to know that through Jesus the forgiveness of sins is proclaimed to you. Through him everyone who believes is justified from everything you could not be justified from by the Law of Moses.'[23]

In other words, by believing and trusting in Jesus Christ they would have right standing before God, something that the Law of Moses could never do. They would be justified and God would choose to see them just as if they had never sinned. This

---

[22] John 3:1-21
[23] Acts 13:38-39

was all made possible because of Christ's sacrifice on the Cross.[24] It is His love outpoured.

PEACE WITH GOD

Billy Graham wrote a book called 'Peace with God' and said, 'God's peace in our hearts is like a spring of pure water that brings cleansing and refreshment to our minds and bodies.'[25] How great is this gift of grace to us; peace in our hearts and much more. The writer of Hebrews says that we can confidently approach God's throne of grace and find both mercy and grace to help us in our time of need.[26] A President may have no time to speak to visitors, but will always welcome a small son or daughter who runs unbidden into his office. How much more will our heavenly Father welcome us.

Derek Prince pointed out that the Greek word for grace in the New Testament is 'charis' which can also mean thankfulness. 'Grace a dieu' means 'thanks to God' and the Italian 'Grazie' and Spanish 'Gracias' - both mean 'thank you.' Let us have both grace and be thankful. There are so many ways that this grace helps and encourages us, giving us hope and comfort. The message of the Cross is able to build us up and give us an inheritance together with all those he has set apart for himself.[27]

There is yet another aspect to grace. Yes, the grace of

---

[24] Romans 3:23-24
[25] Graham, 1984
[26] Hebrews 4:16
[27] Acts 20:32 NLT

God leads us into a family relationship with Christ, which also leads to eternal life with Him. However, God is also looking for a steady growth in spiritual maturity; people who are reliable, obedient, living lives pleasing to God, walking in holiness and enjoying increasing times of fellowship with Him. In other words He is looking for disciples, and this has everything to do with our lifestyle.

Titus was just such a disciple. The Apostle Paul trusted Titus enough to leave him in Crete in order to appoint elders in the Churches, whilst he, Paul, continued on his missionary journey. His letter to Titus, which is found in the New Testament, is full of helpful instructions. Paul sets out the qualifications for leadership and highlights the sound doctrine that Titus should teach. Paul's instructions regarding grace and discipline remain as helpful and pertinent today as they were to Titus. Paul wrote,

'For the grace of God that brings salvation has appeared to all men. It teaches us to say "No" to ungodliness and worldly passions, and to live self - controlled, upright and godly lives in this present age.'[28]

Here the meaning of the word 'teach' is twofold: it is both giving an instruction but also inferring discipline, with reproof, correction, and even chastising.

God displays this love throughout the whole of the Old Testament through His disciplining and chastising of the children of Israel. In the book of Hebrews we read:

'And have you forgotten the encouraging words God spoke

---

[28] Titus 2:11-12

to you, his children? He said, 'My child, don't ignore it when the Lord disciplines you, and don't be discouraged when he corrects you for the Lord disciplines those he loves, and punishes those he accepts as his children.'[29] The teaching we find in the Bible, His Word, has been given for our benefit under the loving hand of our heavenly Father.

A believer will experience great sorrow when the Holy Spirit exposes sin. This sorrow leads to a repentant heart, which is then open to receiving His loving forgiveness. It may be that we have pushed forward with some plan of our own, yet out of His love for us, the Lord shuts the door on it. How glad we are afterwards when we realise the problems we might have endured otherwise.

Just as we know that our own children respond to differing types of discipline, so the Lord knows the best way to correct us. The writer in Hebrews goes on to say how important loving discipline is for a child and although it seems hard at the time, the outcome is good. In the same way, the grace of God works for our own good, in every way possible and always through righteousness and love.

CHRIST'S EXPENSE - the price He paid is beyond our understanding. He, the Eternal King of glory, submitted to being born as a baby, living in a family and working as a carpenter. The sinless Son of God displayed absolute humility, when at the age of around thirty He presented Himself to John to be baptised.

---

[29] Hebrews 12:5 NLT

Jesus' baptism was unique. In Luke's account, we read that John was baptising those who had repented of their sin, yet Jesus was without sin. John recognised this, saying that it was he who needed to be baptised by Jesus. However, Jesus reassured him saying that this act was to fulfill all righteousness.
Whilst Jesus was praying, the heavens opened and the Holy Spirit descended upon Him in bodily form like a dove. A voice came out of heaven, 'You are my Son whom I love; with you I am well pleased.'[30]

From this time on, Christ's Sonship was endorsed through His preaching and teaching, by miracles and the power to forgive sinners. Yet from the very beginning there had been many unique signs. The angel who visited Mary to announce the coming of the Child said that He would be conceived by the Holy Spirit and would be called the Son of God. Joseph was also told in a dream that Mary would bear a Son, who would be conceived by the Holy Spirit. His name was to be Jesus, as He would save His people from their sins. This divine birth would fulfill a prophecy from Isaiah which declared His name would also be Immanuel, meaning 'God with us.'[31]

There is no doubt that these Scriptures are highlighting the fact that Jesus was born the Son of God by the power of the Holy Spirit, confirming Him as 'God with us.' This was no natural conception or ordinary birth.

---

[30] Luke 3:21-22
[31] Isaiah 7:14

JESUS' BIRTH

A group of poor shepherds was given the good news one night as they were guarding their sheep. An amazing display of angels worshipping and praising God left them feeling both disturbed and excited. They then hurried to Bethlehem to find this baby, the promised Messiah.

Wealthy magi, wise men, followed the star to see the new King. They travelled many miles from other countries to worship this small Child who was foretold in their studies, and brought Him gifts of gold, frankincense and myrrh. These gifts were not only important prophetically as they spoke of kingship, worship and prayer, and death, but they were also gifts from God the Father to His Son. Such bountiful gifts would help to sustain the young immigrant family when they reached Egypt a few months later. It is interesting to realise how the Lord prepared financial blessing many months ahead of time for the family and how He will similarly prepare answers to our prayers.[32]

There were also many prophecies in the Old Testament, centuries before Christ's birth. These all gave accurate details of His life, telling for instance the place of His birth in Bethlehem, the ride into Jerusalem on the foal of a donkey, descriptions of His sufferings, even the sharing of His clothes and drawing lots for them at the crucifixion. However, the culmination of the purpose for His life came with His sacrificial death and His resurrection.

---

[32] Matthew 6:8

THE CROSS

The supreme price that Jesus paid came with his sacrificial death on the Cross. In the hours that led up to it, He was rejected by the crowds, then mocked and vilified, spat upon, punched and His beard pulled out by the soldiers. The twisted crown of thorns was placed on His head and the stick they had been beating him with was used to beat the thorns into His head. He was scourged with the leather - thonged whip into which were embedded pieces of bone and metal, tearing his flesh with each stroke.

After this came the walk through Jerusalem with the heavy cross-bar carried on his shoulders. Then came the crucifying; with large nails being driven through hands and feet. At this point all who watched heard him say, 'Father, forgive them for they don't know what they are doing.'[33] This would have amazed the soldiers who were more used to cursing and swearing at this point. It was about nine o'clock in the morning.

Jesus was crucified between two criminals, and from noon until three o'clock in the afternoon, darkness fell. The NIV at this point says that the sun stopped shining. Above and beyond all that He had suffered so far, came the ultimate cost of the price He was paying; He experienced the first and only break in fellowship with His Father as He took the past, present and future sin of the world upon Himself. This caused Him to

---

[33] Luke 23:34

cry out, 'My God, My God why have you forsaken Me?'[34] It was now three o'clock in the afternoon. Jesus asked for a drink and was given wine vinegar from a sponge. Then He cried, 'It is finished!' and gave up his spirit.

The death of the Son of God was such a unique cataclysmic event that even nature reacted. The earth shook, the rocks split, tombs broke open and many holy dead people came to life, later appearing to many in Jerusalem after Christ's resurrection.[35] One can only wonder at the reaction of those who saw 'dead men walking!'

At the Cross the centurion and the soldiers who were guarding Him were terrified. Night had fallen at noon and they had been standing in the dark for about three hours. Now an earthquake shook the landscape. The priests who were ministering in the Temple must have been similarly scared and shocked as the massive heavy curtain (that separated the Holy of Holies from the Holy Place) in the Temple was supernaturally ripped in two from top to bottom.[36] Prior to this only the High Priest could enter into the place of His Presence in the Holy of Holies, and then only once a year. Now God was demonstrating that the way into His presence was open to all through the death of His Son.

However, what was happening as He hung there? It was something that no onlooker could know or imagine. At Christ's enormous expense, He carried our sin upon Himself and

---

[34] Matthew 27:46b
[35] Matthew 27:52-53
[36] Matthew 27:51

became our substitute. A divine exchange was made for all who would turn to Him. He exchanged His righteousness for our sin and our sin for His righteousness.[37] Just as His birth was no ordinary birth, so His death was no ordinary death.

His Sonship was again established and verified when He rose from the dead and further initiated the outpouring of the Holy Spirit on His disciples at Pentecost. All of us who come to Him in faith have salvation and a living relationship with God. We are saved from both the penalty of our sin and God's wrath; saved to eternal life with Him. This is the grace of God.

OUR RICHES

From an eternal viewpoint, our destination after death is vitally important. God has provided a way to spend it with Him through Jesus Christ. The issue is sin. We have an inherited sin nature. Sin comes naturally to us. There is an initial pleasure in sin, but there is price to pay, and dire unsought for eternal consequences. However, Christ has made it possible for us to receive God's forgiveness and this is the message of Easter. He took upon Himself the punishment for sin that was due to us. This is surely the richest gift of all. As we receive Jesus Christ as Lord of our lives, we receive His forgiveness.

Jesus spoke about different types of riches and made a distinction between earthly riches and spiritual one. He urged His listeners to store up spiritual riches rather than earthly ones. Better to have riches that cannot rust, be stolen or be

---

[37] 2 Corinthians 5:21

moth-eaten; spiritual treasures that will be laid up for us in heaven. He was asking people to recognise the driving force in their lives, and went on to say that where our heart is there will our treasure be. [38]

There is so much to grace, and we are so thankful. His grace to us is bathed in His gentleness, His strength, His truth, His power and His righteousness. There is the sweetness of His forgiveness and above all, His love, with the presence of His Holy Spirit - all of this is by His amazing grace. We too can be full of grace because of His unlimited grace to us. We can truly say with Paul, when speaking about Jesus and his grace, 'Thanks be to God for His indescribable gift'[39]

Praise followed. My amazing morning came to an end.

---

[38] Matthew 6:19-21
[39] 2Corinthians 9:15

AMAZING GRACE! how sweet the sound
   That saved a wretch like me.
I once was lost, but now am found
   Was blind but now I see.

'Twas grace that taught my heart to fear,
   And grace my fears relieved.
How precious did that grace appear
   The hour I first believed

Through many dangers, toils and snares
   I have already come.
'Tis grace that brought me safe thus far
   And grace will lead me home.

When we've been there ten thousand years,
   Bright shining as the sun,
We've no less days to sing God's praise
   Than when we first begun.

                John Newton 1725-1807

DAY 2

TRUTH

'Jesus answered, "I am the way and the truth and the life. No one comes to the Father except through Me.' *John 14:6*
'At the length truth will out.' *Shakespeare.*
'All your words are true; .all your righteous laws are eternal.'
Psalm 119:160

AFTER YESTERDAY MORNING and my experience of walking on the Beach I am once more full of anticipation. What will happen today? Will I go to the Beach again and look for another jewel? Yet at the same time I have an inward struggle. Everything seems difficult this morning, heavy, not the easy way of yesterday. Having already been in praise, I turn to my tested source of help - His Word. After reading Psalm 47 which speaks of God, the King of the earth, I then read this verse in the book of Acts which proved to be a key to getting peace;

'But about midnight Paul and Silas were praying and singing hymns to God, and the other prisoners were listening to them. Suddenly there was such a violent earthquake, that the foundations of the prison were shaken. At once all the prison doors flew open, and everybody's chains came loose.'[40] I remembered something that I learned years ago; it is our praise that causes the enemy of our souls to flee, and breaks any spiritual chains that try to hold us. The story of Paul reminded me of this and as I praised, the feeling of 'not getting through' left. The Lord then began to speak;

'Do not strive but relax in Me. Let go of striving. I will show the way this morning. Just rest.'

Straight away I was back on the Beach walking and at peace. I knew I would find another jewel which would connect with His Word. As I walked, a picture of this next stone came to my mind and I saw flashing lights piercing the air ahead. As I walked on they led me to it. It was the diamond that He had put into my thoughts.

As I approached the jewel, I could see its beauty and power. Every facet was sharply cut. Light was flashing from each one against the sky, which I realised was darkening. How it reminded me of the searchlights that were used in World War Two, which lit up the night sky with beams of light looking for enemy aircraft. Then I knew - it was the diamond of truth! I already had the black stone of grace in my hand, but could I or should I, pick up this flashing diamond? The sharp rays of light cut the air towards me as I approached, so I asked the Lord about it,

'What shall I do Lord?'

'Wait. Look at the sea.'

I had been too busy looking at the diamond to notice that the

---

[40] Acts 16:25-26

sea was no longer blue and calm.

'Lord, now the waves look dark and ominous, wild, fierce, strong - a mighty storm is brewing. This is so different from yesterday. What is it all about? It's no longer the lovely sunny Beach I had walked across earlier. What is happening?'

'The sea is the nations - peoples.'

I did not understand and turned to Him for help and He said:

'The sea desires to drown the diamond. But watch.'

I can see that as the sea surges towards the diamond attempting to cover it, a change occurs. The waves become calm and smooth. They gently lap and cannot overcome the diamond. All is peace.

'Even so,' He continued, **'My truth overcomes.'**

Then I wanted to know why it had been so difficult this morning and even as I asked I felt my peace receding again.

'There is warfare over My truth. You are feeling a little bit of it now - hence the difficulty this morning.'

'So I need to have truth with me, in me, at all times Lord. I know Your Word is truth.'

I then asked the Lord if I should pick up the diamond and His reply was, **'You are to wear it.'**

With that the vision faded and I was left with this last amazing statement to contemplate.

It was time to go to the Bible and explore truth.

Truth

We are told in Romans 13 verses 13 -14 to 'clothe ourselves' with the Lord Jesus Christ, but how do we do this? Surely it is a case of first putting off the deeds of darkness, as Paul explains, 'Let us behave decently, as in the daytime, not in orgies and drunkenness, not in sexual immorality and debauchery, not in dissension and jealousy. Rather clothe yourselves with the Lord Jesus Christ, and do not think about how to gratify the desires of the sinful nature.'[41]

Interestingly this is written to the Church in Rome, not to unbelievers. Paul also talks about what to wear in Colossians Chapter 3. We need to clothe ourselves with compassion, kindness, humility, gentleness and patience; bearing with each other, forgiving any grievances we have, and then above all, put on love. Yet how can we fulfil all these attributes?

There are those who seem to be naturally gentle, but can they forgive people who upset them? Others seem loving, but are they humble? We have such different temperaments, some innate, some learned. Surely we are in need of help? To be like Jesus which is our aim, we need to come back to God's grace and His loving power. Only with His help can we wear these clothes. These Godly attributes are supernatural gifts, given through the Holy Spirit, to whom believers have free access.

---

[41] Romans 13:13-14

As believers we can look back and to our amazement realise that the Holy Spirit has been at work in our lives. It is He who has given us victory over certain sins that at one time had been part of our everyday life. No longer do we lose our temper, we are more kind than we used to be and considerate to others. The fruit of the Holy Spirit causes us to have patience, swearing has ceased, and so on. There may be the occasional 'slip up' which we confess to the Lord very quickly, but no longer does it rule us. We know that the new ways of living have come about purely by the grace of God, as the life of Jesus Christ has filled our lives. It is, Christ in us, the hope of glory.[42]

Having said that, there is always further to go! There is a lovely example to consider in the Bible. In the early days when Jesus was calling His disciples, He gave James and John nicknames calling them the 'sons of thunder.' We can only surmise why. Yet when we read the Gospel that John wrote and his three letters we see no longer a 'son of thunder' but a disciple of Jesus who epitomizes love. (Eventually, James his brother was to suffer martyrdom under King Herod Agrippa).

On the night before he died Jesus prayed that His disciples should be sanctified, or made holy, in the truth. His prayer to the Father continued, 'Your word is truth.'[43] Herein lies the key - God's Word. As we begin to walk in the truth of His Word, we find that His grace is always there to help us. We experience the power of the Holy Spirit, and our desire to please the Lord supersedes our desire to please ourselves.

---

[42] Colossians 1:27
[43] John 17:17b

FASTEN YOUR BELT!

When we put our lives into the hands of the Lord Jesus Christ and obey His Word (which is truth), we are in effect putting on truth. It all makes sense, and in putting on truth we are then wearing the belt of truth, part of our spiritual protection. This is described in Ephesians 6 as our 'spiritual armour.' Any Roman soldier not wearing his belt was considered undressed for action. The belt held the sword, and there would often be strips of leather hanging from the belt to give protection for the lower body. Without his belt and sword, he was vulnerable to the enemy's attack. We are likewise vulnerable if we do not wear the belt of truth.

The writer of Ephesians, Paul the Apostle, spent much time in prison chained to Roman soldiers and no doubt began to get a greater understanding of spiritual armour from the Holy Spirit during these times. Truth must be foundational in our lives and it will bring us protection as it did with Jesus.

TRUTH FOR TODAY

Truth has almost become a lost virtue. Advertisements and the promises they make can be misleading. Half-truths can give a totally false impression, which happens with biased media reporting. Photographs can be manipulated to tell a different story and modern film making techniques brilliantly present the impossible as reality. However, any half-truth is a lie.

In the area of beliefs and truth, what we believe becomes truth for us. So, one person's concept of the truth may be different from another's, even on the same topic. Good and bad is looked on as being relative with no absolutes. So it would appear that everybody is allowed to have his own valid idea and opinion in a free society, which for him will be truth, and he will live his life by it. (Not so in a totalitarian state where deviation from the expressed system can result in death or imprisonment.)

However, in his book 'Against The Flow', Professor John Lennox says the following,

'The trend to relativize does not end with religion. Indeed, once you think about it, you realize that any relativizing tendency inevitably affects values and ultimately even truth itself.'[44] He goes on to talk about the way that post-modernism expects us to accept as absolute truth, that there are no absolute truths, and in that way contradicts itself. 'The fact is that no-one can live without a concept of absolute truth.'[45] He continues pointing out that any red figures in our bank account would be counted as absolute truth by any bank manager.

When we are looking at Jesus Christ and God's truth, we see absolute truth that obeys His standards and conforms to His laws. Good and bad are defined by Him. How many of us learned at school that the atom was the smallest particle and could not be split? Scientists proved this wrong and a new devastation entered the world. What was considered to be truth was found to be false. If we consider that science is the discovery and understanding of God's creation, there may be new revelations that contradict previous statements.

---

[44] Lennox p38, 2015
[45] ibid p39

There is an interesting scene in John Chapter 18 where Jesus and Pilate meet. The Jews wanted to put Jesus to death but had no authority to do this under their own Law. Their recourse was to approach the Roman Governor Pontius Pilate hoping to be able to implement the Roman death penalty. Pilate wanted to know what accusation they had against Jesus and because they couldn't give him a straight answer he decided to ask Jesus himself. He began with the crucial question; 'Are you the King of the Jews?'

Now so far as Rome was concerned there was only one king and that was Caesar, so the 'correct' answer to this was essential. But Jesus answers Pilate with a question, 'Are you saying this on your own initiative, or did others tell you about Me?' Pilate retorted that he was not a Jew; he was not the one bringing Him to trial. It was in fact Jesus' own people. Jesus then made a statement that belies some of the aspirations found amongst Christians today. He replied that His kingdom was not of this world. Had it been, His subjects would be fighting for His release.

'So you are a king!' declared Pilate, whereupon Jesus said: 'You say correctly that I am a king. For this reason I have been born, and for this I have come into the world, to testify to the truth. Everyone who is of the truth hears My voice.'

Pilate continued by asking a question that even today philosophers debate, 'WHAT IS TRUTH?' He then went out to the crowd and said to them, 'I find no fault in Him at all.'

Shortly afterwards Pilate publically and symbolically washed his hands of all personal responsibility. Nevertheless politics caused him finally to submit to the Jews' demand when the sovereignties of Christ and Caesar clashed. 'We have no king but Caesar,'[46] called the chief priests in front of him, as the crowd screamed for His death; with that Pilate made his decision. He could not appear to acknowledge any other king or god but Caesar, so he acquiesced and had Jesus prepared for crucifixion with flogging.

It is interesting to read in secular history that after this, Pontius Pilate persecuted the Jews in many different ways. One such event was described by Josephus, an early Romano-Jewish historian. Pilate was ordered to erect images of Tiberius Caesar in Jerusalem, an act which outraged the Jews whose laws did not allow images to be set up, and a riot started. Pilate of course sent in the troops, and much bloodshed followed. In this case Caesar was obviously not acknowledged as the king of the Jews. Eusebius, a later historian, quoting Josephus commented, 'Now if you compare this with the account in the Gospels, you will see that it was not long before their own cry came back to haunt them, when they shouted before Pilate that they had no king but Caesar.'[47]

Josephus then related another massacre by Pilate. He had spent Temple funds to help build an aqueduct and anticipating trouble, Pilate stationed disguised soldiers amongst the crowd, armed with clubs. When the uproar started, he gave the signal and the soldiers used their weapons killing many Jews, others being trampled to death as they fled. Pilate was eventually recalled to Rome to answer to many allegations, but

---

[46] John 19:15
[47] Maier, 1999

Tiberius Caesar died before he arrived and he found himself under the rule of Caligula. History records that he then chose to commit suicide, so his comment 'What is truth?' may have been something that had haunted him.

GOD'S TRUTH

The Old Testament has much to say about truth. It is one of the foundations of God's teachings and His expectations for the believer. When David asked the Lord God about this, He replied emphasising our relationships with each other,
'LORD, who may dwell in Your sanctuary?
Who may live on Your holy hill?
He whose walk is blameless and who does what is righteous,
Who speaks the truth from his heart, and has no slander on his tongue,
Who does his neighbour no wrong and casts no slur on his fellow man.'[48]

The Psalm of David goes on to praise the one who after making a promise also keeps it, even if it then proves a disadvantage to himself. How many times are we let down by somebody who has made a commitment and suddenly finds a 'better' option has come his or her way.

---

[48] Psalm 15:1-3

TWO DIFFERENT MEN

When King David was challenged by Nathan the prophet over his adultery with Bathsheba and the murder of her husband (who was one of his mighty warriors), he did not try to lie his way out of the situation. Instead he confessed the truth and repented. God called David 'a man after His own heart.'[49] King Saul on the other hand tried to manœuvre his way out of all blame when Samuel confronted him on a matter of disobedience.

Saul had just fought and been victorious over the Amalekites and had been instructed by the Lord to destroy all that belonged to them including Agag the Amalek king. However, Saul and his people decided to keep the best of the animals and everything else they found of value. Samuel and Saul met after the conquest. Saul was happy and blessed Samuel, saying how he had carried out all the words of the Lord. But Samuel had only to look around and listen. Then he knew that Saul had not obeyed the Lord's instructions. He had just one question and we can well imagine the inquiring tone of his voice.

'What then is this bleating of sheep in my ears, and the lowing of oxen that I hear?'[50]

Saul is caught out and prevaricates saying that 'the people' (not he) had kept the best of the sheep and oxen in **order to sacrifice**

---

[49] Acts 13:22
[50] 1Samuel 15:14

them to the Lord. In other words he was acting from the best of intentions. Samuel however gave God's verdict,

'Does the Lord delight in burnt offerings and sacrifices,
as much as in obeying the voice of the Lord?
To obey is better than sacrifice,
and to heed is better than the fat of rams.
For rebellion is like the sin of divination,
And arrogance is like the evil of idolatry.
Because you have rejected the word of the Lord,
He has rejected you as king.' [51]

Then Agag, who had also been spared, cheerfully and confidently joined the two men thinking that he had escaped death. But it was not so and Samuel succeeded where Saul had failed, putting him to death with a sword. The outcome for Saul was the loss of the kingdom, which then passed to David.

Has the Lord changed? Can we exchange obedience for sacrifice? Sometimes we find it easier to be sacrificial than to obey Christ. We will give money, our time or anything, rather than follow God's Word. We think we are pleasing God in this way and possibly earning our salvation. However, Jesus, who was always obedient to His Father, said that if we love Him we will keep His commandments. Our giving will come out of our obedience.

In returning to truth, we find God's words on it spoken by the prophet Zechariah,
'But this is what you must do: Tell the truth to each other.

---

[51] 1Samuel 15:22-23

Render verdicts in your courts that are just and that lead to peace. Do not make evil plots to harm each other. And stop this habit of swearing to things that are false. I hate all these things.' says the Lord.[52]
Many years earlier the prophet Isaiah had said this,
'Woe to those who call evil good, and good evil,
who put darkness for light and light for darkness,
who put bitter for sweet and sweet for bitter!'[53]
Now doesn't this remind us of something that is prevalent today? God says, 'Woe to them.'

Many times the Lord God pronounces 'woe' in Scriptures; for instance we find examples in the writings of the Old Testament Prophets, and again in the New Testament Gospels. In Luke's Gospel we read of many pronouncements of 'woe' by Jesus, mostly against the religious leaders who were hypocrites. The situation arose when Jesus was invited to dinner by a Pharisee who had been listening to His teaching. The man was surprised to see that Jesus did not wash before his meal, but he did not anticipate Jesus' strong reply. Jesus pronounced 'woe' on the Pharisees who were more interested in the outward act of washing their hands than on keeping their inward life clean. Six more 'woes' followed, each one highlighting the hypocritical ways of the Pharisees and the Lawyers. Each time this word was an expression of God's disfavour with dire consequences to follow.

God is looking for truth in all areas of our walk with

---

[52] Zechariah 8: 16-17 NLT
[53] Isaiah 5:20

Him. Children think that 'fibs' are unimportant and are acceptable. Adults rarely acknowledge exaggeration to be lying. But let us remember that Jesus said that we will all stand before God for every word we have spoken.[54] Lying can be the habit of a lifetime yet is one of those things that can also be totally healed by repentance and the power of the Holy Spirit. Let us also remember that when we repent, He not only forgives but washes us clean of all unrighteousness.

The Lord also looks for our worship to be both in spirit and in truth.[55] What does this mean? Surely it is a matter of the heart. Whenever and wherever we worship He is looking at our heart. The Westminster Shorter Catechism of 1648 had succinct questions and answers to help people learn Bible truths, and it makes interesting reading. Martin Luther used this catechism to educate children and help them to better understand Bible faith. They would have learned the words by rote, giving the answer to each question. The first two questions and answers are good to ponder over:

Q1. WHAT IS the chief end of man?
A. Man's chief end is to glorify God and to enjoy Him forever.
Q2 WHAT rule hath God given to direct us how we may glorify and enjoy Him?
A. The Word of God which is contained in the Scriptures of the Old and New Testaments is the only rule to direct us how we can glorify God and enjoy Him.

---

[54] Matthew 12:36-37
[55] John 4:23-24

THE PILGRIM'S PROGRESS

There is a lovely character in this famous book written by John Bunyan called Mr. Valiant- for-Truth. Did he get his name from Jeremiah Chapter 9 verse 3?
'And like their bow they have bent their tongues for lies.
They are not valiant for truth on the earth.
For they proceed from evil to evil,
And they do not know Me, says the Lord.'

In the story we meet Valiant-For-Truth standing covered in blood, sword in hand. He is talking with Great Heart having previously fought Wildhead, Inconsiderate and Pragmatik single-handed for three hours; fighting as always for truth. Great Heart commented that he must have become really weary fighting for such a long time. Valiant replies, 'I fought till my sword did cleave to my hand, and when they were joined together, as if a sword grew out of my arm, and when the blood ran through my fingers, then I fought with most courage.' [56] Valiant was on his way to the Celestial City. He had previously heard Mr. Tell-True describe the glories of it, relating Christian's battles as he too had journeyed there. Valiant said that his heart had fallen into a burning haste to go after him, and even though his parents had done all they could to dissuade him, still he got away and started on the journey. Eventually, having overcome many discouragements and stumbling blocks, the time came for Valiant to cross the river.
'He left his sword for whoever would succeed him in his

---

[56] Bunyan, 1965, p259

pilgrimage, and as he went into the water, said, "Death where is Thy sting?" And as he went down deeper, he said, "Grave where is thy victory?" So he passed over, and the trumpets sounded for him on the other side.'[57]

Time for me had also passed - too quickly, and I heard the Lord say; 'Now go to sleep My child. Wear truth.'

---

[57] ibid p276

Prophetic Word

Hear this Word My child, My children.
You know to draw near to Me, and I will draw near to you.
Learn how to draw near in all situations, at all times, for all reasons. Learn how to know My voice and hear Me even when I whisper.
Know how to spend time in My presence. Break through the warfare and wiles of the evil one who always tries to prevent you. Allow Me to lead and guide you in all things, for My ways are perfect. Do not be led astray by whims and fashions even in 'spiritual' ways. My ways are simple and easy and not complicated.
Trust My word at all times. Have faith and believe. Be ready for the times that are coming and nearly upon you. In Me you are safe and in Me you will be filled with joy and My love.
Know that you, My precious children, are upon My heart at all times. My dear, dear, children, My Son died for you. This is My love shown to you.

DAY 3

THE BLOOD OF CHRIST

'The New is in the Old concealed and the Old is in the New revealed.'
Augustine
'In Him we have redemption through His blood, the forgiveness of sins,' *Ephesians 1:7-8*

Yesterday had started off with a struggle. It was quite a battle to get to that place of peace and the realisation of nearness to the Lord. But today is a new day! I am so glad He wakes me up for our times together. And now to come boldly into His presence, I enter straight into praise and worship, not hurrying, taking my time to draw near to His throne of grace.
'Lord you have given me the black stone of Your grace, and the diamond of your truth to wear. I am already overwhelmed and yet I know there is more. Help me Lord.'
Immediately I find that once more I am on the Beach. It has happened so quickly. No struggle today. I'm walking over the pebbles - looking. It is such a lovely place of peace. All is calm. It is a balmy day. As I walk I begin to know in my spirit that I will be looking for a deep, dark red jewel and that this will be the stone of the blood of Christ.
'Lord this revelation has come so swiftly from You. There is no

striving needed this morning. I know that this new jewel will remind me of the blood of Christ.

As I continue walking and searching amongst the pebbles, I easily find the blood red stone that the Lord had told me about. It stands out. It is dark red and clear - a wonderful jewel. I can see into it.

'The Blood Stone! What shall I do with this stone Lord? It is such a precious and beautiful jewel.'

I pick it up and look at it. As I hold it, blood runs from it - all over my hands. It cleanses the work of my hands. I lift the stone to my mouth. It cleanses the fruit of my lips. The blood of Christ is for all of me - to be forgiven - to cleanse hidden sin - to wash me clean inside and out - no part missing and it is for my body's healing. Later I was to discover this in Proverbs 12 verse 14,

'From the fruit of his lips a man is satisfied with good things as surely as the works of his hands rewards him.'

I find I am almost trembling as I look at the stone and begin to understand more fully its impact. As I hold this precious jewel it is as if I am being overwhelmed by God's love. This is also a sobering time. How can mere words explain what I am seeing and experiencing? I am being impacted by the most dynamic and unparalleled event in world history: the full force and significance of the Son of God shedding His blood for all mankind defies reason. Perhaps the acceptance of the words leads to more understanding as the Holy Spirit brings revelation. I know that the Word of God will have much to say about this, so, to the Study. The vision fades.

The Blood of Christ

THE INTRODUCTION or 'first mention' of many doctrines and themes of the Bible are found in the first book of the Bible, the book of Genesis - the 'Book of Beginnings'. We find the theme of 'blood' running right through both the Old and New Testaments. The Old Testament speaks of the blood of animal sacrifices for the covering of sin and the New Testament continues with the sacrificial Blood of Jesus Christ for the forgiveness of sin.

THE FALL OF MAN

Our first ancestors Adam and Eve lived in the most perfect of settings. The Garden of Eden was the most beautiful and glorious home one could imagine. They had all that they needed and each evening the Lord God their Maker walked and talked with them. There was perfect friendship and fellowship between them and one can only wonder at their conversations.

The garden was full of trees that provided fruit and food for Adam and he could wander at will and eat, but there were two very special trees in the midst of the garden. There was the 'tree of life' and the 'tree of the knowledge of good and evil.' Adam could eat freely from the first but the second tree was forbidden and held a severe warning. The Lord said that if he ate from it, he would die on that day. It was sometime after this warning that we learn of the creation of Eve, a lovely companion and helpmeet for Adam. It was she who was tempted by Satan, as he questioned God's motives and poured doubt on His Word.

'Has God said...?' purred Satan, causing doubts to rise in Eve's mind. She listened to Satan's beguiling words. Was God withholding something that would increase her wisdom and knowledge? Did God really say they were not to eat any of the fruit in the garden? She knew the answer to that question; it was just one particular tree that was forbidden. But would they really die? Satan knew what she was thinking,

'You surely will not die! God knows that in the day you eat from it your eyes will be opened, and you will be like God, knowing good from evil.[58]

In this one forceful statement, Satan planted in her the lie that God would not judge her disobedience; she could eat and there would be no consequences, no penalty, she would not die. In other words, she could get away with sin and disobedience to God's command and He would not judge her. All would be well. Perhaps He did not really mean it. Perhaps God prevaricates?

How prevalent is this belief now in the 21st Century amongst some Christians. The thought is that God is love (which He is) and only love, (interpreted as man's version of love) and would therefore never judge our sins. However, when we read the Bible we know that God is also righteous and holy

---

[58] Genesis 3:4-5

and must judge sin.

There are many examples to verify this. A very severe and thought provoking one is found early in the book of Acts Chapter 5. Ananias and Sapphira, who were part of the early Church, chose to sell a piece of property in order to bring the proceeds to the disciples. However, they kept part of the money for themselves but maintained they had brought the total amount. Peter first challenged Ananias who stoutly repeated the lie then fell down dead. Three hours later his wife Sapphira arrived and not knowing what had previously happened, confirmed the lie. She too then breathed her last and was buried next to her husband. It is no surprise to read the Bible's comment, that great fear came over the whole Church and all who heard of it. The issue was that they had lied to God and tested the Spirit of the Lord. Do we?

The loving grace of God does not mean we can deliberately go on sinning. However, it does teach us that He has provided forgiveness for those who repent and turn away from sin. This indeed is the message of the Cross, but to take as a belief that God never judges is to be mistaken and to be easily deceived. 'Sin isn't sin any more,' is the lie, and 'everyone else does it,' does not make it right. There will come the time when we will all stand before God and have to answer to Him for our behaviour.

Satan continued tempting Eve, intimating that God knew that if she ate the fruit her eyes would be opened and she would become like God herself. This of course was something that Satan so desired for himself. So, she thought, God was trying to deprive her of Godly status, added to which, the fruit looked delicious and it would give her wisdom.[59] She looked. She took. She ate, and gave some to Adam.

After eating the forbidden fruit there was an immediate consequence; their spirits, the part of them that communicates with God, died. Their bodies no longer immortal began the process of dying. Death happened on that very day as God said it would and it also resulted in a visible change; they realised that they were naked. So uncomfortable was this that they tried to make coverings for themselves. Previously they had been naked and innocent, but now they had a practical knowledge of evil, and in this first act of disobedience, experienced guilt on their consciences, and felt uncovered. Sin, having begun with disobedience was now taking root.

We can't say for sure, but had they been covered with the glory of God before they ate? All we know is that they were now naked, their consciences had been corrupted and in trying to rectify this, they made clothing from fig leaves. Then they heard the steps of the Lord coming nearer and did something they had never done before. They hid. The close fellowship and loving friendship that they had enjoyed was now lost and they were experiencing fear. The Lord called out, 'Adam, where are you?' Of course the Lord knew where they were, but did they know where they were, spiritually speaking? Do we?

In the conversation that followed and in the subsequent events, they began to understand the seriousness of their disobedience. They came to realise that they and all future generations would be affected by the knowledge of good and

---

[59] Genesis 3:6

evil. Also the earth and everything belonging to it fell under the curse, producing amongst other things, thorns and thistles, sickness and disease. And war. In future, man would have to work hard to eat.

The Lord made clothes of skins for them to replace their own temporary method of covering and they were banished from the Garden forever. Eventually they would die physically. Of course, their new coverings meant the death of an animal. So here we have the first instance of blood being shed to provide a covering for mankind's sin. Centuries later this first sacrifice was finally consummated by Christ for all mankind.

IT GOES ON... AND ON...

The repercussions from this first rebellion percolated into Adam's family and have continued throughout the generations ever since. Man's new sin nature was established and soon manifested itself in Adam's family. The time came when his two sons brought offerings to sacrifice to God. Abel brought a first born lamb, but Cain brought something he had grown from the ground, which had been cursed and was therefore unacceptable to God.

At this rejection Cain's face darkened with anger. He heard the Lord warning him that sin was crouching at the door and wished to have him, 'But you must master it,' said God.[60] What followed was more shedding of blood, but this time it was Abel's blood as he was murdered by Cain. God faced Cain

---

[60] Genesis 4:7c

asking him of his brother's whereabouts and then it was that Cain uttered the much quoted statement,
'Am I my brother's keeper?'[61]

It is inconceivable that Adam had not told his sons about the Garden of Eden and the reason for the banishment. They would have heard how God provided their parent's covering by shedding the blood of the animal, yet only Abel had obeyed this precedent and brought the acceptable sacrifice. Man cannot satisfy God in his own way. It has to be His way.

LET MY PEOPLE GO

Many generations later, when the importance of the blood sacrifice was well established, God called Moses to go before Pharaoh and plead for the release of the enslaved Israelites. God was saying through Moses, 'Let My people go!' yet Pharaoh kept refusing. Consequently a most devastating series of plagues and disasters hit Egypt in a matter of months, one after the other. Each one was a message from Almighty God to Pharaoh. Each one showed His mighty omnipotence over the Egyptian gods. Each one brought fear and dismay to the people.

The god of the River Nile was impotent to overturn God's judgment when He turned the water to blood. All the streams, ponds and reservoirs were similarly affected, the fish died and the smell was appalling. The frog god was shown helpless when a plague of frogs hit Egypt. The Egyptians liked

---

[61] Genesis 4:9

to worship the frog, but now they had millions of them hopping around, in their beds, in their ovens, in their food, everywhere. Then came the gnats, as prolific as dust on the people and their animals, these were followed by flies, vast swarms of them everywhere. Next and in one day all the Egyptians' livestock in the fields died, and just as they were sorting this out, everybody began to be afflicted with boils.

After this came the most severe storms ever experienced with hailstones so large that it was dangerous to be outside. Trees were felled and the farmers' ripe barley and flax crops were ruined. Then came the locusts, there were so many that the ground could not be seen for them. Anything green that remained was eaten.[62] Then darkness fell and covered the land leaving the Egyptians housebound for three days.

What was this all about? God had instructed Moses to ask Pharaoh's permission for the Israelites to go into the desert, where they would be free to worship Him. Hundreds of years earlier, when Joseph, son of Jacob had welcomed his father and family into Egypt they had been free to worship. But as the families of Israel multiplied, new Pharaohs became afraid of their numbers, and as a result they were enslaved. Pharaoh knew that to grant Moses' request would mean the end of his slave labour force and he was not prepared to allow this. First he said 'yes' as the plagues did their damage and then he said 'no' as Moses interceded and God stopped the problem. Pharaoh's magicians and all the people were emotionally exhausted by this and pleaded with him to let the Israelites go.

---

[62] Exodus 7-10

They had had enough - but not Pharaoh. He still prevaricated and in so doing crossed the line of God's patience and forbearance, making way for His divine wrath to be shown.

THE DOOR

The Israelites remained untouched by God's judgments and this did not go unnoticed by the Egyptians. But now the line had been crossed and the final plague was about to descend which again would not affect the Israelites if they followed God's instructions. It would also be the doorway to their freedom. Passover was about to be introduced.

Moses called for all the elders of Israel and said to them, 'Go and take for yourselves lambs according to your families, and slay the Passover lamb. You shall take a bunch of hyssop and dip it in the blood which is in the basin, and apply it to the lintel and the two doorposts; and none of you shall go outside the door of his house until morning. For the Lord will pass through to smite the Egyptians; and when He sees the blood on the lintel and on the two doorposts, the Lord will pass over the door and will not allow the destroyer to come into your houses and smite you.'[63]

The Israelites were to take a year old lamb (or goat, which was acceptable) that was unblemished and after keeping it from the tenth day of the first month until the fourteenth day, it was to be killed. Some of its blood was to be put on the two doorposts and lintels and then the roasted meat was to be eaten

---

[63] Exodus 12:21-23

inside the house along with unleavened bread and bitter herbs. The Lord would pass over every house that had blood on the door and death would not enter. Those without the sign of the blood would suffer the death of their first born sons and animals.

And so it was. The Israelites obeyed God, following all His instructions. Just after midnight the sound of weeping and wailing filled the land as families found death in their homes. Pharaoh also found his own firstborn son dead. At last, he not only agreed to let them go but could not get them out quickly enough. Moses had pre-warned the people to eat the meal fully dressed and eat it quickly as they would be leaving Egypt in a hurry. The Egyptians plied them with treasures of all kinds: jewelry, gold, silver, clothing, fabrics, metals and spices, pleased that they were leaving and hoping it would signal the end of all their troubles.

Thus the Feast of Passover was introduced as the angel of Death passed over the Israelites. This was to be remembered and celebrated over the centuries and would be established as one of the three annual Jewish Feasts to be celebrated in future years in Jerusalem.

THE PASSOVER LAMB

Just hours before Christ was crucified, He celebrated 'The Passover Meal' with His disciples which we may know as 'The Last Supper'. The disciples sat with Jesus and celebrated the freedom from slavery and the saved lives of the early Israelites through the sacrifice of blood. As they ate and drank from the various cups of wine, Jesus revealed to them the spiritual significance of this present Passover feast, a feast that had been celebrated for so long in Israel. Now it was to evolve into a celebration of freedom from the slavery of sin, with eternal salvation for souls through the blood of the Lamb of God.

The door into this freedom was Jesus Christ Himself. Thus the New Covenant was instituted, the first being taken away in order to establish the second.[64] It was also a way for all believers in future to remember His sacrifice.
'While they were eating, Jesus took bread, gave thanks and broke it, and gave it to the disciples, saying, "Take and eat; this is My body." Then he took the cup, gave thanks and offered it to them, saying, "Drink from it all of you. This is my blood of the new covenant, which is poured out for many for the forgiveness of sins."'[65]

Jesus was to be the fulfillment of all the Old Covenant sacrifices. The fellowship offering, the guilt offering, the sin offering, the peace offering, the burnt offering, the grain offering and the trespass offering, all taught in the book of Leviticus, were accomplished and fulfilled in Christ's one sacrifice; Jesus – the Messiah, the Lamb of God.

---

[64] Hebrews 10:9
[65] Matthew 26:26-28

WHY BLOOD?

Why is blood so important? The book of Leviticus gives us the answer to this. The issue is that shed blood leads to death. 'For the life of any creature is in its blood. I have given you the blood so you can make atonement for your sins. It is the blood representing life that brings you atonement.'[66]

The righteous penalty for sin is death, so the blood of an innocent animal was shed to pay that debt. A life for a life - but only the perfect life of the Son of God could bring life for all mankind. Only then could Satan's domination that started in the Garden be overthrown. The whole of the Old Testament was leading up to this, the redemptive plan of God. All of the Old Testament is foundational to the New. Once more, as Augustine had said, the 'Old' is in in the 'New' revealed.

REDEMPTION

The Priests and Levites of the Old Testament were not allocated any territories in the Promised Land. Instead they were to receive portions of meat, grain, olive oil and the finest wine from the offerings brought to God. Also, the first born of all animals and sons were to be offered to them, but when the baby boys were a month old the parents were to 'buy back' their sons by paying five shekels of silver to the priests.[67] In this way the matter of redemption was introduced, a payment for a life. Their sons were 'bought back.'

---

[66] Leviticus 17:11 NLT
[67] Numbers 18:14-16

Today we can understand redemption in a different context. There are more and more pawnshops on our streets where people can get a money loan in exchange for some precious object. If later they can raise the cash, they can 'redeem' or buy back their watch or necklace or whatever they had pawned. But our redemption is an eternal matter,

'For you know that it was not with perishable things like silver or gold that you were redeemed from the empty way of life handed down to you from your forefathers, but with the precious blood of Christ, a lamb without blemish or defect.'[68]

There is yet a further way that the blood of Christ is effective in our lives. Sometimes even after repenting we still have the lingering feeling of guilt. We know we have been forgiven but we still have a guilty conscience. What are we to do? Again the Word comes to our aid like a sword. The blood will cleanse our conscience, and as we claim the power of the blood in prayer, declaring this truth, we will find relief;

'How much more, then, will the blood of Christ, who through the eternal Spirit offered himself unblemished to God, cleanse our consciences from acts that lead to death so that we may serve the living God!'[69]

Gerald Bridges says in 'The Discipline of Grace' that the only way we can relate to God is through the blood and righteousness of Jesus Christ.[70] It is only the blood that will cleanse us from a guilty conscience and give us the confidence

---

[68] 1Peter 1:18-19
[69] Hebrews 9:14
[70] Bridges, 1994, p22

to enter the presence of God.[71]

ATONEMENT (AT-ONE-MENT)

The High Priest of the Old Testament entered the Holy of Holies once a year in order to bring atonement to Israel and to himself. Now, as believers we have the privilege and the right to enter into God's presence whenever we pray. We have 'at-one-ment with God,' that is, reconciliation, being 'at one' with Him, through the blood of Christ.[72]

JC Ryle, who became the first Anglican Bishop of Liverpool and who died in the year of his retirement in 1900, gave this sobering instruction;[73]

'I charge you never to give up on the doctrine of the blood of Christ, the complete satisfaction which that atoning blood made for sin, and the impossibility of being born saved except by that blood. Let nothing tempt you to believe that it is enough to look only at the example of Christ, or only to receive the sacrament which Christ commanded to be received, for which many nowadays worship like an idol. When you come to your deathbed, you will want something more than an example and a sacrament. Take heed that you are found resting all your weight on Christ's substitution for you on the Cross, and His atoning blood or it will be better for you if you had never been born.'

---

[71] Hebrews 10:19-22
[72] Romans 5:11
[73] Ryle, 1970, p108

The Lord spoke to me again,
'Now My child I have been silent this morning- but actually you have heard Me speaking to you all morning through My Word. You know that when you take in My Word you are hearing Me speak. So rest now. You have had a good feast this morning.'

That was so true and marked the end of a special time.

WHEN I SURVEY THE WONDROUS CROSS
On which the Prince of glory died,
My richest gain I count but loss,
And pour contempt on all my pride.

Forbid it, Lord, that I should boast,
Save in the death of Christ my God:
All the vain things that charm me most,
I sacrifice them to His blood.

See from His head, His hands, His feet,
Sorrow and love flow mingled down:
Did e'er such love and sorrow meet
Or thorns compose so rich a crown.

Were the whole realm of nature mine,
That were an offering far too small,
Love so amazing, so divine,
Demands my soul, my life, my all.

Isaac. Watts 1674-1748

DAY 4

THE KINGDOM

'Jesus said, "My kingdom is not of this world."' *John 18:36a.*
'Your kingdom come. Your will be done on earth as it is in heaven.'
Matthew 6:10
'But seek first his kingdom and his righteousness, and all these things will be given to you as well.' *Matthew 6:33*

TODAY AFTER A TIME in praise and worship I was aware that the next time that I went to the Beach, I was to look for a pearl. This pearl would have something to do with the kingdom of God. It seemed that the Lord was calling it the pearl of great price, which brought some scriptures to my mind like Matthew 13 verses 45 and 46,

'Again, the kingdom of heaven is like a merchant looking for fine pearls. When he found one of great value, he went away and sold everything he had and bought it.'

Then I asked Him in prayer,

'Lord what am I to do with the pearl when I find it?'

'My child you may pick it up. It is your most treasured possession.'

'Lord, teach me about this treasure, the pearl.'
'So look in My Word. It is all there. Seek it out. Search for it. This pearl is to be searched for most diligently.'
I needed the Lord to lead me.

Then I found myself walking along the Beach again. I was looking for the pearl, but not having much success. Pebbles yes, pearl no! My mind too was still full of our conversation.

'Lord I have started to find out about this pearl from Your Word but I am not finding the pearl.'
This is because you have to really seek the pearl. My kingdom is hidden, yet to the seeker it is revealed. It is My gift to you. When you seek it-then it shall be found.'
'So Lord, it is not lying on the Beach like the other three stones?'
'Seek and you shall find. First find the large rock. The pearl is not amongst the pebbles. Find the large rock, the massif, you will find the pearl there.'

So I walk along the Beach, and this time I am looking for a very large rock. Ahead I see a vast, dark outline against the sky and walk towards it. I have found the rock. Amazingly I see a man standing there and I know it is Jesus. As I walk towards Him I get the impression that He wants me to lay 'my all' down before Him. I know He wants to give me the pearl. I approach Him. Then we continue to talk: He tells me that He has all my concerns in His hands and I can trust Him.

'Yes Lord with your help I give my cares to you. Does this mean that the pearl is mine in exchange for giving You all my cares?'
'No. The pearl became yours when you picked up the blood stone. You had already acknowledged Me as your Saviour and King, repenting of your sins and walking in new life. With your new life given by the blood, you entered the kingdom. In

coming to Me the Rock, you are in the kingdom and the pearl is your prize possession My child. Now walk in kingdom ways. It is the good and fair land.'

I began to realise that it is the King that I need to seek. In seeking and finding Jesus, the King, I am finding the kingdom.

Once more the Beach faded away and I went to the Word of God.

The Kingdom

'For He rescued us from the domain of darkness and transferred us to the kingdom of His beloved Son.'   *Colossians 1:13*
'Jesus began to preach, "Repent, for the kingdom of heaven is near."'
Matthew 4:17
'The Kingdom of God is the sovereign rule of God.'
T. Austin -Sparks

I FOUND IT VERY ENCOURAGING, that in the vision I had been directed to a great rock, and there found the Lord. It reminded me that Christ had referred to himself as the great Rock when speaking with the Apostle Peter.

One day Jesus asked His disciples who people thought He was. They answered that some thought He was John the Baptist. (Herod himself thought He was John the Baptist come back to life after being beheaded.) Other people thought Jesus was Elijah or Jeremiah or one of the other prophets. Then Jesus said, to His disciples, 'But who do you say I am?' At this, Simon Peter burst out, 'You are the Messiah, the Son of the Living God.' Christ then turned to him saying that His Father in heaven had revealed this truth to him, and went on to give Simon son of Jonah a new name: Peter, 'Petros,' 'a little rock.' He continued saying that He would build His Church on 'petra,' *this* rock, the massive bedrock of Peter's statement. He, Jesus was the Rock on which the Church would be built and the gates of Hades would not overpower it.[74]

The Old Testament held a foreshadowing of this statement, as the word 'rock' was used numerous times when talking about or describing God. For example, in the early verses of the song of Moses we find this,
'For I proclaim the name of the Lord:
Ascribe greatness to our God.
He is the Rock, His work is perfect;
For all His ways are justice,
A God of truth and without injustice;
Righteous and upright is He.'[75]
Many will remember the chorus 'Ascribe greatness to our God the Rock.'

The Apostle Paul wrote of Christ as 'the Rock' Who had accompanied the Israelites when they were travelling towards the Promised Land. 'They all ate the same spiritual food and drank the same spiritual drink; for they drank from the spiritual rock that accompanied them, and that rock was Christ.'[76] Thus 'The Old is in the New revealed.'

WHAT AND WHY

WHAT IS THE KINGDOM of heaven like and why is it so important? The earlier words from Colossians Chapter 1 and verse 13 give a succinct answer: There is the domain or the dominion of

---

[74] Matthew 16:13-18
[75] Deuteronomy 32:3-4
[76] 1Corinthians 10:3-4

darkness, and there is the kingdom of God. We are in one or the other. These are spiritual truths which as well as being a reality now will be manifested in eternity. God's kingdom is our desire.

THE WAY IN

We have some idea about worldly kingdoms. For instance Queen Elizabeth is a Constitutional Monarch, the United Kingdom being ruled through a democratically elected Parliament. Yet there are countries whose kings hold absolute power and whose word is law. (There are also despots who rule their lands in the same way.)

Jesus said to Pilate at His trial that, yes He was a king but His kingdom was not of this world. As we understand the United Kingdom by living in it, so the kingdom of God is one to be experienced in order to begin to understand it. Eventually the time will come when Jesus returns and then His Kingdom will be of this world.

At the start of His ministry Jesus Christ's first words to the people were, 'Repent for the kingdom of heaven is at hand.'[77] The whole of His life on earth was a demonstration of kingdom precepts. Wherever He went, He, the King, taught all who would follow Him the new ways of the kingdom. These demonstrated the grace, the holiness and the righteousness of God.

For us, the way into a worldly kingdom is by birth or application for citizenship. However, the way into the kingdom

---

[77] Matthew 4:17

of God is via Jesus Christ and the Cross, with repentance leading to new birth or being 'born again.'

Crowds had already been flocking to John the Baptist to be baptised because he too had been preaching exactly the same message. The ordinary people welcomed this but sadly the majority of the religious elite, the Pharisees, Scribes and Sadducees rejected his words, and the message of Jesus as Messiah.

Even so, the people came in their thousands to Jesus to both hear all He had to say and to be healed from their sicknesses and diseases. 'Jesus went throughout Galilee, teaching in their synagogues, preaching the good news of the kingdom, and healing every disease and sickness among the people.'[78]

Some months later Jesus sent His disciples out to the towns and villages to do the same thing. They were to proclaim the Gospel of the kingdom and with His authority heal the sick.[79] This commission has not changed and is passed on to Christ's disciples today. After His resurrection, He instructed the disciples in kingdom practice; to preach the Gospel, make disciples, baptising them and teaching them all He had commanded. The kingdom signs of healing and deliverance from demons would accompany the Word.[80]

When we read of the kingdom in the Gospels we find that two distinct terms are used, the 'kingdom of God' and the

---

[78] Matthew 4:23
[79] Luke 9 and 10
[80] Mark 16:16-18

'kingdom of Heaven'. Theologians have debated whether they are interchangeable in meaning or not. We learn from the late Dr. Robert Lindsey, co - founder of the Jerusalem School of Synoptic Research, that the Pharisees were so afraid of taking the Lord's name in vain (one of the Ten Commandments), that they did not write or use the word 'God' lest they broke this Commandment. Instead they would speak of the kingdom of Heaven. From this point of view it would seem that the two are interchangeable and we know that many Jews today, including Messianic believers, do not write the word 'God' for the same reason, preferring 'G - d.'

There is an alternative interpretation. The kingdom of God is seen as the eternal kingdom, which stretches from eternity to eternity, the kingdom of Almighty God. But the kingdom of Heaven is that portion of the kingdom of God, which is from Christ's first coming until His second advent.

WHAT IS THE KINGDOM LIKE?

In the second year of His ministry, Jesus started to teach about the kingdom using parables. These were familiar stories which had a hidden meaning, mysteries that the world would not understand but which would be revealed to those who choose to follow Him. These early disciples began to understand that only those who wanted to follow Jesus fully would have the truth revealed to them and Jesus always made time to explain the meanings to them.

He spoke some parables to the crowds, some only to the disciples and some were directed to the Pharisees and other

Temple leaders. This first one He spoke to the crowds who followed Him and His disciples. He was by the Sea of Galilee and the crowd was so large that He needed to speak to them from a boat. He told a parable about a farmer who went out to sow his seed. As he scattered the seed by hand, it fell on different types of ground. Some seed fell on the side of the road and the birds came down and ate it, some fell on stony ground where there was no depth of soil, so the plants did not develop. Other seed fell in the thorn bushes and started to grow but were entangled by the thorns and had stunted growth. However some seed fell in good, rich soil and grew to produce a crop, some a hundred fold, some sixty and some thirty. [81]

This scene would have been very familiar to the local people but the disciples wanted to know the underlying meaning. What was Jesus really telling them? So they approached Him about it, and He explained it by describing four different kinds of people and their reactions on hearing the Word of God. He said that the seed was the word of the kingdom and the differing types of soil represented the hearts of people who heard His word. 'There are those,' said Jesus, 'who don't understand the word of the kingdom and the little they do know is snatched away by Satan.' This seed had fallen on the roadside and the birds came and ate it up.

Next there are those who are really enthusiastic about what they hear and appear to have understood the word and are going on well. However, when troubles or problems or persecutions come, they give up, they have no root in

---

[81] Matthew 13:1-23

themselves. Just like the seed which fell in stony places, there was no depth. Then there were those who having heard have started off well but the thorns of worldly worries and the desire for wealth overtook their life, and they lost interest. None of these seeds would develop and come to harvest, but the final picture is of the person who receives and understands the word of the kingdom, and is faithful. He is good soil and is fruitful.

Mark in his Gospel account adds that Jesus said if they did not understand this parable how would they ever understand all the others? So it was vital that He explain it to them. In effect, this first parable is a key to all the others. Are we good soil? Are our hearts fully receptive to God's Word whether we are a new believer or a mature one. He speaks to us throughout our lives and each time the condition of our heart will test the progress of ongoing maturity and faith.

Jesus continued to tell the crowd another parable which warned them that not everyone would be found in the kingdom. There was a farmer who sowed his field with wheat and whilst his farm helpers were asleep, his enemy came and sowed darnel (tares) amongst the wheat. This was a weed that resembled wheat in the early stages but as the two grew and the wheat matured, the differences were obvious, darnel being a type of ryegrass. His men wanted to pull out the weeds but the farmer said 'No,' as in so doing they would uproot some of the best crop. It was best to wait until harvest was ready and then the weeds could be gathered together and burned and the wheat harvest put into his barns.

The crowds were all still there on the beach listening to Jesus - they had never heard teaching like this before. He

The Kingdom

continued with other parables that showed the power of the kingdom. It may seem small at first but it has outstanding growth as has been proved, for to this day Christ's message is filling the world and changing lives. After sharing these parables He and the disciples left the crowd and went into the house where He was staying. Now that they were on their own they wanted to know the meaning and relevance of the wheat and tares.

He said that the field is the world, the one who sows the good seed is the Son of Man, and the good seed are the sons of the kingdom. The tares are the sons of the evil one and the enemy who sowed them is the devil. The harvest is the end of the age, and the reapers are angels. Just as the tares are gathered up and burned with fire, so shall it be at the end of the age. The Son of Man will send forth His angels, and they will gather out of His kingdom all those who commit lawlessness, and will throw them into the furnace of fire where there will be weeping and gnashing of teeth. Then the righteous will shine forth as the sun in the kingdom of their Father. Jesus ended with a favourite saying, 'He, who has ears, let him hear.' [82]

As they were absorbing this He brought other parables, encouraging them, showing them that His kingdom was exceedingly precious. It was the best thing they could desire. He went on to say that the kingdom was like treasure which a man found in a field. He hid it and then sold all he possessed to buy the field. The kingdom was also like a merchant who was seeking fine pearls, who when he found one that was

---

[82] Matthew 13:37-43

exceptional sold all he had to buy it.

Jesus then returned to the theme of the wheat and the tares, but this time with a parable to appeal to the fishermen in their midst. He said that the kingdom of heaven is like a net that is thrown into the sea and catches all kinds of fish. When it is full the net is dragged to the beach and the fish examined. The good fish are kept and stored and the bad fish are thrown away. As with the wheat and the tares, at the end of the age the angels will come, take out the wicked from among the righteous and will throw them into the furnace of fire and there will be weeping and gnashing of teeth. This last phrase is so graphic, drawing a picture of remorse, regret, sorrow, hate and horror.

Then Jesus asked them if they had understood what He was saying and when they replied 'Yes' Jesus continued by saying, 'Therefore every teacher of the law who has been instructed about the Kingdom of heaven is like the owner of a house who brings out of his storeroom new treasures as well as old.'[83] The lawyers of Jesus' time were in a sense the university post graduates of the Mosaic Law and the sacred writings. They were the ones who would be called on to examine the difficult or finer points of the law. If they became disciples, how much greater would be their understanding and ability to teach.

Jesus is saying that not all will enter the kingdom, yet time and again in His ministry, He gave an open invitation into eternal life. In speaking to Nicodemus, He emphasised that eternal life is for all who will believe and keep on believing in

---

[83] Matthew 13:52

Him. He was the only who could offer them salvation. [84] This very belief leads to repentance and is the key that opens the door to new life and knowing the incredible love of the Father.

There was a time when the disciples must have been asking each other who would be the greatest in the kingdom. When they approached Jesus about it, He called a child forward and said that unless they were converted and became like little children they would not even get into the kingdom of heaven. As for being great in the kingdom, it was the one who humbled himself as a child. He was not looking for childishness, but that childlike quality found in the very young. Little children are not arrogant, they believe easily, they like to please and they love and trust whole heartedly. There is a delightful innocence about them and they are also greatly loved by the Lord. This trusting quality is prized in the believer.

On one occasion the disciples were disciplined by the Lord over this very matter. They were trying to stop the mothers with their babies and children from reaching Jesus, but He rebuked them publicly saying that the kingdom belongs to such and that whoever did not receive the kingdom of God like a child would not enter it at all.[85]

Standing in the crowd and listening to this was a wealthy young man, a ruler, who wanted to know what he should do to inherit eternal life. Jesus replied by taking him through some of the Ten Commandments, the issues of adultery, murder, theft, perjury, and honouring his parents, to which the man answered

---

[84] John 3
[85] Luke 18:17

in the affirmative. He had kept all these from a young age. Then Jesus put His finger on the one thing that ruled this ruler, his wealth! Jesus told him that just one thing was lacking, 'Sell all that you possess and distribute it to the poor, and you shall have treasure in heaven; and come, follow Me.'[86]

Not only did Jesus highlight this one stumbling block, but in doing so He was also showing this man that he was failing to keep the first two commandments, to 'have no other god before Me' and to 'have no idol nor worship or serve them.' His wealth, his money and his position were his gods and he could not give them up. He so wanted to 'do' something to earn a place in the kingdom. Had he let go of his treasure, he would have discovered Jesus Himself was in fact his treasure and the answer to his question. Jesus was giving him the same invitation that He had given to Peter, Andrew, James and John, Levi and the others. When He called them they immediately left their businesses and followed Him.

This man could have been one of them with the extra promise of treasure in heaven. But sadly, the price was too high to pay and he went away in grief.

Interestingly Jesus did not call him back and we do not know if this wealthy man ever repented from his decision, a man of whom the scripture says, 'Jesus loved'. Jesus commented to those watching that it was hard for the wealthy to get into the kingdom. It was easier for a camel to get through the eye of a needle, but He continued, 'The things that are

---

[86] Luke 18:18-23

impossible with people are possible with God.'[87]

The disciples who had left all to follow Jesus then reminded Him of this and said in effect, 'Well what about us? We have left everything'. Here is His reply;

'Truly I say to you, there is no one who has left house or wife or brothers or parents or children, for the sake of the kingdom of God, who will not receive many times as much at this time and in the age to come, eternal life.'[88]

Not everyone has this calling on their life, but those who become disciples will find that there is a 'leaving' of their old way of life which family and friends may not understand. In some countries and faiths this will mean that they are cut off from their family, persecuted or even killed.

It is also interesting to note that as soon as Jesus had said this to them He began to tell them of the great price that He was about to pay; the mocking, spitting, mistreatment, scourging, and death by crucifixion. But He emphasised that He would rise from the dead three days later. The disciples understood none of this.

TO DO OR NOT TO DO

Jesus gave some further insights into the kingdom when He began to talk to the people about the Law (the Teachings), which as Jews they would have been taught by the Pharisees and the Rabbis. However, He astounded them by saying that they

---

[87] Matthew 19:26
[88] Luke 18:29b-30

would not get into the kingdom unless their righteousness exceeded that of the Pharisees. Their 'righteousness' consisted of legalistically interpreting and meticulously keeping laws to an extreme.[89] The way they did this exhibited a self- righteousness which later Jesus condemned. He called them hypocrites, saying they were like tombs painted white that looked beautiful but which were in fact filled with dead men's bones and putrefaction.[90]

At this point the disciples may have started to feel that this was not their problem. After all they were not like the Pharisees! But Jesus then raised the standard even higher by showing them that there was a vast difference between God's standard and man's standard of righteousness. He began to explain: the kingdom is a kingdom of holy righteousness. Everyday actions like anger, mental lust and adultery were not kingdom ways. He went on to list conspicuous generosity, lack of forgiveness, worry, judging another's sin whilst practicing it, hidden sins that only God knew of; all this and more fell short of the righteousness that He looked for. This would have filled them with dismay. Who could measure up to these standards?

Later, when they were filled with the Holy Spirit at Pentecost they would understand that Christ's own righteousness given in exchange for their sin was the answer. Paul expressed it like this,

'God made him who had no sin to be sin for us, so that in him

---

[89] Matthew 5:20
[90] Matthew 23:27-28

we might become the righteousness of God.'[91]

Jesus Christ took our sin upon Himself at the Cross in order that we might be made righteous. Consequently, when we go before God to worship or to pray, He sees us as righteous.

This outstanding gift is given to us. Does this gift of grace given so freely mean that believers can carry on sinning to their hearts content? The Apostle Peter addresses this by reminding us of God's requirement of holiness,

'As obedient children, do not conform to the evil desires you had when you lived in ignorance. But just as he who called you is holy, so be holy in all you do; for it is written, "Be holy, because I am holy"'[92] Jesus would later teach the two commandments that would fully encompass all the commandments: to love God with all your heart, all your soul, all your mind, and to love your neighbour as yourself.[93] Keeping just these two would cover the keeping of all the Ten Commandments, likewise the breaking of just one of the ten would equate to breaking the whole law.[94]

WHO IS YOUR FRIEND?

When the Pharisees and the Scribes saw that Jesus was attracting the tax gatherers, and the sinners, they started to grumble. He was having meals with them, giving them a lot of

---

[91] 2 Corinthians 5:21
[92] 1 Peter 1:16
[93] Matthew 22:36-40
[94] James 2:10

attention, talking with them, befriending them. These were people that they, the leaders and upholders of the law, would disdain to know. But Jesus had a different attitude, so He told them the parable of the shepherd who had a hundred sheep.

When he found there was one sheep missing, he left the ninety-nine and went to find the one that was lost. He put it on his shoulders, told all his friends he had found his one lost sheep and they all celebrated and rejoiced together. This parable was relevant to the Pharisees so Jesus explained it to them,

'I tell you that in the same way there will be more rejoicing in heaven over one sinner who repents than over ninety-nine righteous persons who do not need to repent.' How enraged they were as they realised Jesus was highlighting their self- righteous failure to see their need for true repentance, but commending these sinners who did repent.[95]

There are many parables of the kingdom mostly found in Matthew's and Luke's Gospels. In all of them Jesus recounted real life situations that they understood: farming, fishing, building construction, wedding arrangements, family life, vineyard culture, land letting, business management and practices, finances - all had a place in the stories Jesus told. There was something for everybody, with an aspect of kingdom life to be drawn out of each parable. These practical applications drew the crowds and the truly interested ones discovered their deeper significance.

---

[95] Luke 15:7

WHEN THE KING RETURNS!

Subsequent kingdom parables related to His second coming. Jesus and His disciples were talking together on the Mount of Olives, just a few days before the crucifixion. They would have had a good view of Jerusalem and the Temple, as they asked Jesus about the signs of the end of the age and His coming again. Jesus answered by predicting many significant events that would take place and giving them severe warnings to always be ready for His second coming. Again He spoke in parables, the first one being the parable of the five wise and five foolish virgins.[96]

Ten bridesmaids were waiting for the bridegroom to come so that they could go in with Him to the wedding feast. They all had their lamps trimmed and filled with oil, but because the bridegroom came much later than they had anticipated, they all fell asleep. In the middle of the night there was a shout! The bridegroom was coming. The wise virgins who had brought extra oil were able to relight their lamps but the foolish ones had not and had to go and buy some.

By the time they got back, the wedding party had moved into the banqueting hall and the door was locked. 'Lord, open the door for us,' they called but he replied that he did not know them. Jesus then warned His listening disciples, 'Therefore keep watch, because you do not know the day or the hour.'[97] We too do not know the day or the hour when He is coming back and need also to be on the alert and ready. Today we are surrounded

---

[96] Matthew 25
[97] Matthew 25:13

by signs warning that He is coming back soon.

Oil is often a symbol of the Holy Spirit in the Bible. Not only do we need to be alert, but also to be prepared. As the wise virgins not only had their lamps filled with oil, but also took an extra supply, so too we need to be constantly filled with the Holy Spirit. In the parable, a lack of oil was the reason for the five foolish virgins being shut out of the wedding feast.

The book of Revelation describes this marriage feast, telling us that those who are invited to it are blessed,
'Hallelujah!
For our Lord God Almighty reigns.
Let us rejoice and be glad
and give him the glory!
For the wedding of the Lamb has come,
and His bride has made herself ready.
Fine linen, bright and clean,
was given her to wear.
(Fine linen stands for the righteous acts of the saints.)
Then the angel said to me, "Write, 'Blessed are those who are invited to the wedding supper of the Lamb!'" And he added, "These are the true words of God.'"[98]
This is an invitation that we should desire. We need to be ready and prepared for the coming of Jesus.

---

[98] Revelation 19:6b-9

BORN AGAIN. (AGAIN?)

Modern advertising agencies have picked up on this phrase and have sometimes talked about their product in this way. For example; we can have 'born again' cars, jeans or even soap. The phrase has been used so much and in such a way that has sullied and demeaned its true glorious meaning.

Jesus spoke with Nicodemus, an influential Pharisee who had come to Him by night to ask Him some questions. He wanted to find out more about this 'Man' who was not only teaching with authority but healing people too. Jesus declared, 'I tell you the truth, no-one can see the kingdom of God unless he is born again.'[99]

We tend to interpret this conversation through the Gentile tradition, assuming that Nicodemus did not understand the concept of being born again. However, looking at it through the tradition of Judaism we can see that there is another way. As a Pharisee, Nicodemus would be well versed in the concept of being born again. Judaism taught that there were several ways to be born again, but each one having a physical connotation. For instance, being born of water was a rabbinic idiom for natural birth and to be born a Jew under the Mosaic Law was one way to be born again.

Other ways of being born again included being baptised for ritual cleansing where full immersion was expected. At the age of twelve or thirteen all Jewish boys entered adult life, which was another way of being born again. Getting married which led

---

[99] John 3:3

into a new life of responsibility was another way. Anyone converting to Judaism would mean being born again and a king of Israel was said to be born again on entering that office.

Nicodemus was puzzled. Surely he was qualified already. Did he have to start all over again? But it was impossible. He could not start his life again by going back into his mother's womb. What was this Godly Man, Jesus talking about? Jesus then went further and taught him that God required a spiritual rebirth. To be born again was an action of the Holy Spirit, not something that one 'did' and it could only be accomplished in the believer's life by believing on the Son of Man. He referred Nicodemus back to a situation in the Old Testament that he would have known well.

The Israelites had been grumbling and complaining on their journey through the desert, wishing they could go back to Egypt. God therefore sent a plague of poisonous snakes which caused great distress and many deaths. Moses did what Moses always did; he went to the Lord who instructed him to make a bronze snake and put it on a pole for all to see. God explained to Moses that all those who looked to the bronze snake when bitten would live.[100]

Jesus continued to say to Nicodemus that in the same way that Moses lifted up the bronze snake onto the pole, so too the Son of Man would be lifted up and whoever believed in Him and kept on believing would have eternal life. Nicodemus would have then understood Christ's meaning. He, Jesus, would be lifted up in crucifixion and all who looked to Him

---

[100] Numbers 21:9

when 'bitten by sin' would live.

Nicodemus must have become a follower of Christ. We read in John Chapter 19, that he and Joseph of Arimathea took on the task of un-nailing Jesus' body from the Cross, cleaning and wrapping the body in strips of linen with anointing spices and placing it in Joseph's new tomb. A large stone was then rolled across the tomb to seal it. Surely Nicodemus would have remembered his first conversation with Jesus the Messiah during these hours. So much loving faith was now in this man. To do what he did, touching a dead body, especially at the time of the Passover would have officially excluded him from worship according to Jewish Law. Instead he ministered to Jesus Christ, the King of kings.[101]

Many people now claim to be born again Christians. When a person is truly born again there will be radical change as they are filled with the Holy Spirit. Their lives will never be the same again and this will be evident to those around them. The Apostle Paul expounds the new birth explaining that when we are born again it means just that; we die to our old self and become new people in Christ as He lives in us. Paul states that all who were baptised into Christ Jesus were baptised into His death, buried with Him through baptism into death so that just as He rose from the dead so we rise into new life.[102]

This is so pictured in the act of baptism, the going down under the water into death so to speak, and coming up again into the new life. This is an enactment of something that has

---

[101] John 19:38-42
[102] Romans 6:4

already happened in the life of the believer. The new life has already come through repentance and faith in Christ. For all who desire a new life and an end to the past - Jesus is the Way.

'Therefore, if anyone is in Christ, he is a new creation; the old has gone; the new has come!'[103]

EATING AND DRINKING?

Paul described the kingdom like this,
'...for the kingdom of God is not a matter of eating and drinking, but of righteousness, peace and joy in the Holy Spirit.'[104]

This was written to the Church in Rome and Paul was replying to a problem that had arisen. The Christians were of both Jewish and Gentile backgrounds and their different cultures brought different interpretations to Christian lifestyle. Food was the topic. Gentiles enjoyed their food and drink and nothing was unclean to them. The Jews had used certain foods and wine in their sacrifices in order to obey the Law and certain foods were unclean, forbidden, to them.

The context in which Paul was writing was the issue of not putting a stumbling block before a brother. To provide food for a brother who believed it was unclean would cause him to stumble and damage his conscience. If he believed it was unclean, then to him it would be unclean, even if you, as host, believed it was not unclean. Better to be sensitive and walk

---

[103] 2 Corinthians 5:17
[104] Romans 14: 17

according to love and not hurt him.[105] 'Kingdom ways are not food and drink but rather righteousness, peace and joy in the Holy Spirit,' said Paul.[106]

These ways are the hall-marks of Christian living. All that we need to enter and to live the life is given to us freely. All we can give is ourselves.

ON THE MOUNTAINSIDE

When Jesus had been teaching what we call the Beatitudes on the mountain side (sometimes called The Beautiful Attitudes), He continued by telling them a little more about life in the kingdom. They were not to worry about the basics of life. Jesus assured His disciples telling them, 'Your Father knows what you need before you ask Him.'[107] 'So do not worry, saying, 'What will we eat?' or 'What will we drink?' or 'What will we wear?' For the pagans run after all these things and your heavenly Father knows you need them. But first seek his kingdom and his righteousness, and all these things will be given to you as well. Therefore do not worry about tomorrow; for tomorrow will worry about itself. Each day has enough trouble of its own.'[108]

Jesus was teaching all the disciples that their prime concern was their relationship with God, seeking kingdom life first and putting worldly concerns second. Likewise for us

---

[105] Romans 14:14-15
[106] Romans 14:17
[107] Matthew 6:8
[108] Matthew 6:31-34

today, the King is aware of our concerns and will make sure we get what we need. We need to get our priorities right. In the West, it is the acquisition of wealth that reigns. In the kingdom of God it is trust in the King that counts. In our lives, He reigns.

The Lord and I began to talk again.
'Lord is there a sense in which the pearl is a combination of the black stone, with the diamond and the blood stone and perhaps more?'
'A mystery child but one which is open to revelation as you keep seeking and keep finding.'
'Then Lord, I need to keep seeking and finding and that is a whole new study.'
'More a lifetime My child.'

And with this my morning ended.

Prophetic Word

My dear, dear child, there is always a 'now' time to come into My presence, to hear My voice and be prepared for all that I require. Dear child, as you are prepared, so I prepare you. In this we work together. So hear Me My child. Let me give you warnings and allow Me to speak these things into your heart. Learn from the past and from My Word. Events move swiftly world-wide, and those with great power and authority in the world already are making their moves towards calamity. But you My child, My children, are not to fear and not to begin to fear. All is in my hands, in My sovereign power, and all is in My grace too. There will be a growing differentiation between the sons of the Kingdom and the sons of the evil one. My sons will see this and become aware too. Keep your eyes on me and you will not fear the waves and the storm, and you will find that I AM all that you need in all and every situation. Did I not cause thousands to eat to full satisfaction from such a little? Did I not part the seas for My people to both escape from danger and escape into My situations? So don't be alarmed or fear, as I AM all that you need. But be prepared, watch, wait and pray at all times and I will lead you on.

Glory

DAY 5

GLORY

'Grace is but glory begun, and glory is but grace perfected'
Jonathan Edwards
'The heavens declare the glory of God...' *Psalm 19:1 NKJV*

THIS MORNING THE LORD asked me if I was weary of gathering stones on the Beach. I replied that my concern was to always have His choice of how we would spend our time together, rather than my own. Then the Lord asked me to decide and He would approve my choice. To the Beach of course! So it was with great delight that we went back to the Beach.

The vision opened and I was walking along at the water's edge. He continued, saying to me;
'Today you are going to look for sapphires.'
'Sapphires? More than one Lord?'

Then the Lord reminded me of the time that I had seen sapphires of many different colours on display in a jeweler's window in Spain. There were sapphires of different shades of blue, of gold, yellow, green, lavender and pink. And I had thought all sapphires were blue!

'So go, look, My child. This morning is going to be fun. You see My child; there is variety in the colours of the sapphires that I have made. Each colour is beautiful and pleases Me, yet is still a sapphire. You think of blue only, but I have shown you that there are other colours.'
'You are the Lord of infinite variety. All lovely.'
'So go, and look.'
'Can I pick them all up?'
'Remember the manna -pick only the ones you require. They will show My glory.'
'Then I shall have one of each colour Lord?'
'You've got it!'
    I was swiftly on the Beach again, with the freedom to find sapphires of many colours and learn of God's glory - wonderful! I walked on and on, remembering the various colours of sapphires in my mind as I continued looking. Then the vision faded. This was strange as I was not aware of gathering the jewels but I knew that somehow I had done so and they were mine.

After that I was eager to get into the Study to look up scriptures about sapphires and God's glory......

God's glory - the essence of the presence of God.

Glory

THERE IS A WONDERFUL DESCRIPTION in Exodus Chapter 24 verses 9-11 of a meeting between God and Moses, Aaron and his sons, and seventy elders of Israel. They went at God's invitation to the top of Mount Sinai, but only Moses was given permission to approach God. The others were to worship at a distance and the people themselves were not to even step on to the mountain. Nevertheless, the elders all met, ate and drank in His presence and saw under His feet a sapphire pavement.

'Moses, Aaron, Nadab, and Abihu, and the seventy elders of Israel, went up and saw the God of Israel. Under his feet was something like a pavement made of sapphire, clear as the sky itself. Yet God did not raise his hand against these leaders of the Israelites; and they saw God, and they ate and drank.'[109]

It is easy to assume that the sapphire pavement was blue, yet just as the sky can be many different colours, pale green, lavender, pink, orange, yellow, purple and many shades of blue, so can sapphires. So what colour was the pavement? How appropriate that in this vision the Lord chose the sapphire to show something of His glory! This description also completely enlarged my understanding of the sapphire pavement under God's feet and the integrity of God's Word,

---

[109] Exodus 24:9-11

for 'blue' is not mentioned in this Exodus quotation. Perhaps the pavement was a changing vista of colours. Whatever it looked like, it must have been an amazing experience, not only to see Him but also to fellowship together with Him over a meal. Would they have been in the presence of the pre-existent Jesus Christ?

The International Colored Gemstone Association (ICGA) writes this about the sapphire. 'In earlier times, some people believed that the firmament was an enormous blue sapphire in which the Earth was embedded. Could there be a more apt image to describe the beauty of an immaculate sapphire? And yet this gem comes not in one but in all the blue shades of that firmament, from the deep blue of the evening sky to the shining mid-blue of a lovely summer's day, which casts it spell over us. However, this magnificent gemstone comes in many other colors: not only in the transparent greyish -blue of a distant horizon but also in the gloriously colorful play of light in a sunset - in yellow, pink, orange, and purple. Sapphires really are gems of the sky, although they are found in the hard ground of our blue planet.'[110]

After that awesome time together, Moses and Joshua went further up the mountain to meet God privately. Here Moses received both the Ten Commandments on stone tablets, and detailed instructions for the building of the Tabernacle and everything connected with it.

The Tabernacle was a tent, which was to become the first place that these ex-slaves could call their own worship

---

[110] InColour Magazine ICGA

'building.' It was divided into three sections and in the last section, the Holy of Holies; the Lord God would make His presence known to the High Priest once a year. This portable 'pre Temple' went with them throughout their long season of wanderings in the wilderness and prefigured the future magnificent first Temple built by Solomon in Jerusalem many years later.

Moses was with God on the mountain for forty days and as the people below looked towards the summit, they saw the Lord's glory looking like a 'consuming fire.' It must have been an awesome sight and probably quite frightening. This begs the question, having experienced all this, how could they only days later have demanded that Aaron make an idol, a golden calf, so that they could worship it? They even donated their gold earrings. Maybe we can ask similar questions of ourselves, when after experiencing His great love and presence in an amazing way, we later fall into unbelief.

The Israelite people were not unfamiliar with seeing the glory of the Lord. From the beginning of their journey from Egypt to the Promised Land, the Lord had given them a pillar of cloud to lead them by day and a pillar of fire to lead by night. There were occasions when the glory of God was revealed to them in the cloud. For instance there was the time when they had been grumbling and seriously complaining to Moses and Aaron about the lack of food, saying they wanted to go back to Egypt. The Lord then intervened, saying that He was going to provide both bread and meat for them. 'While Aaron was speaking to the whole Israelite community, they looked towards the desert, and there was the glory of the Lord appearing in the cloud.[111]

God also showed His glory at this second confrontation. Three men, Korah, Dathan and Abiram incited two hundred and fifty prominent Israelite men to rebel against Moses, saying in effect that Moses was no more holy than any of them. They were all holy, so why was he giving all the orders and taking the leadership? God rose to the challenge, and vindicated Moses and Aaron in a devastating and most spectacular way to be found in Numbers Chapter 16. But interestingly, God Himself showed His glory at these times of confrontation.

In this next situation, Moses asked God to show him His glory. This came as a result of a deep personal conversation with the Lord and a desire to see more of Him. However, the Lord replied that He would show him His goodness; Moses would not be able to see His face for no-one could see His face and live. Instead he was to stand on a rock and when His glory came Moses was to shelter in a crevice of the nearby rock, thus being allowed to see only the back of the Lord as He passed by.[112] This event inspired the writing of the old hymn 'Rock of Ages cleft for me, Let me hide myself in Thee,' by Augustus Toplady in 1776.

Would Moses have remembered that previous time when the Lord passed over the Israelite homes in Egypt, saving the lives of their first born? This time the Lord was showing Moses His goodness, granting his request and keeping him safe.

---

[111] Exodus 16:10
[112] Exodus 33:12-23

THE HIGH PRIEST'S JEWELS

The sapphire was one of the twelve stones used to adorn the Jewish High Priest's breastplate of judgement. Each stone was engraved with the name of one of the twelve tribes, so figuratively the High Priest would carry the people over his heart, as our High Priest Jesus does with us. God gave Moses detailed instructions for the making and design of the breastplate when he was on the mountain top:

'Fashion a breastplate for making decisions - the work of a skilled craftsman. Then mount four rows of precious stones on it. In the first row there shall be a ruby, a topaz and a beryl; in the second row a turquoise, a sapphire and an emerald; in the third row a jacinth, an agate and an amethyst; in the fourth row a chrysolite, an onyx and a jasper. Mount them in gold filigree settings.'[113]

In this way we see the importance given to the twelve tribes. Not only were their names engraved on the jewels of priestly garment, but when we see the description of the New Jerusalem, we find that their names were also written upon the gates of pearl in the Holy City Jerusalem.[114]

The names of the twelve Apostles of Jesus Christ are also given important prominence. Their names were written on the twelve foundations of the wall of the Holy City, the New Jerusalem.[115]

It is also interesting to compare the similarity between

---

[113] Exodus 28: 15a, 17-20
[114] Revelation 21:12
[115] Revelation 21:14

the following two sets of jewels: the jewels on the High Priest's garments and those found in the foundations of the New Jerusalem as described in Revelation Chapter 21 verses 19-20. With all of these details, the link between the special calling of Abraham's family, the Jews, in the Old Testament and the calling of Christ's apostles in the New Testament is easily seen.

The Jewish connection is unmistakable. To get into the Holy City, one must walk alongside its great high wall. This was built on twelve foundations, each one named with one of the twelve Apostles of Jesus Christ. Entrance was through one of the twelve gates, each one named with one of the twelve tribes of Israel. Jesus Himself said that salvation is of the Jews.[116] The Apostle Paul wrote that God's gift and His call are irrevocable and the time would come when all Israel would be saved.[117]

The description of the New Jerusalem which will be on the New Earth, with its broad street of pure gold like transparent glass, is quite wonderful.[118] In times past, many were told that the streets of London were paved with gold and those who took it literally were greatly disappointed when they went there. But the City of God is quite a different matter.

---

[116] John 4:22c
[117] Romans 11:26a,29
[118] Revelation 21:21b

THE NAME ON THE SAPPHIRE

'Simeon' meaning 'to hear or discern' (implying obedience, contentment, understanding and witness), was engraved on the sapphire of the High Priest's 'breastplate. Simeon was one of Jacob's twelve sons, all of whom became the leaders of the twelve tribes of Israel. Jewish parents often chose names for their children, the meaning of which they hoped would be significant in the child's life or nature. There are times when the name given would be prophetic. Jesus added another name to His disciple Simon, calling him Peter, (Petros) 'the little stone or rock.'

We may also be given a new name if we remain faithful in this life and are what the Bible terms 'overcomers.' Jesus gave this promise, 'He who has an ear, let him hear what the Spirit says to the Churches. To him who overcomes, I give some of the hidden manna. I will also give him a white stone with a new name written on it, known only to him who receives it.'[119]

So what is an overcomer? I believe every born again Christian who learns to hear and be obedient to God's Word is an 'ovecomer' - remaining faithful to the end. Do we always 'overcome?' Sadly no, and this is usually because we choose to do things 'our way' not His. However, when we do overcome, tasting victory and recognising the amazing answer to prayer, we certainly know about it.

One of the most significant situations in which we can overcome is that of dealing with the sin which so often presents

---

[119] Revelation 2:17

itself. Thankfully we have the promise as Christians that we are no longer under sin's mastery and we now have the power to say 'No.' Paul explains it like this, 'Our old sinful selves were crucified with Christ so that sin might lose its power in our lives. We are no longer slaves to sin. For when we died with Christ we were set free from the power of sin.'[120]

Sin will not be a problem in eternity.

THE RADIANCE OF THE FATHER'S GLORY

One day Jesus took Peter, James and John for a walk up a mountain. They had no idea what was coming, for Jesus was entirely and supernaturally transfigured in front of them. His clothes became radiant and whiter than any laundry could achieve.[121] Later in his Gospel and referring to this, the Apostle John wrote that they had seen Christ's glory saying, 'And the Word became flesh, and made his dwelling among us. We have seen His glory, the glory of the Only Begotten Son, who came from the Father, full of grace and truth.'[122]

The writer of the book of Hebrews describes Jesus as being 'the radiance of the Father's glory,' one of the loveliest phrases in the Bible.[123]

Will we see His glory? Yes we will, according to Romans 8 verse 18. The Roman Christians were suffering under Caesar, and Paul writes to encourage them not to give up, telling them

---

[120] Romans 6:6-7 NLT
[121] Matthew 17:1-3
[122] John 1:14
[123] Hebrews 1:3

that the sufferings they are going through are not to be compared to the glory that they will see in the future. So yes, we too will see His glory; it was Jesus' prayer:

'Father I want those you have given me to be with me where I am, and to see my glory, the glory you have given me because you loved me before the creation of the world.'[124]

It would seem that God shows His glory in many different ways - is this why the Lord chose sapphires?

EZEKIEL SEES

Ezekiel the prophet was taken in vision to see some amazing and prophetic scenes. In Ezekiel Chapter 1, he describes a vision of God. First of all he saw four living creatures, quite unique beings, and over their heads was an expanse that seemed to sparkle like ice. Then came a voice! Still looking, he saw what looked like a throne with the appearance of a sapphire, and on the throne was the appearance of a man with fire and brightness of light all around him.

'Above the expanse over their heads was what looked like a throne of sapphire, and high above on the throne was the figure like that of a man. I saw that from what appeared to be his waist up he looked like glowing metal, as if full of fire, and that from there down he looked like fire; and brilliant light surrounded him. Like the appearance of the clouds on a rainy day, so was the radiance around him. This was the appearance of the likeness of the glory of the Lord. When I saw it, I fell face

---

[124] John 17:24

down, and I heard the voice of one speaking.'[125]

It is a picture that an artist might try to paint, and not fully succeed, but surely the Lord has included it in His Word so that we can have some idea of His glory. This vision introduced Ezekiel to his mission of speaking God's words to the rebellious Israelites.

ISAIAH HEARS

Isaiah the prophet heard the Lord say that the time would come when everybody would see His glory,
'Every valley shall be raised up,
every mountain and hill made low;
the rough ground shall become level,
the rugged places a plain.
And the glory of the Lord will be revealed,
and all mankind together will see it.
For the mouth of the Lord has spoken.'[126]

The glory of Christ's second coming, as He comes to bring judgement on the unrighteous and salvation to His own will be a delight to the righteous and a fearful time for the unrighteous. Jesus said, 'Therefore keep watch, because you do not know on what day your Lord will come….So you also must be ready, because the Son of Man will come at an hour when you do not expect him.'[127]

---

[125] Ezekiel 1:26-28
[126] Isaiah 40:4-5
[127] Matthew 24:42,44

CREATION'S GLORY

There are ways in which we see the glory and the power of God in His creation; the beauty of flowers, mountains, animals, roaring seas, volcanic eruptions, lightning, sunsets, forests, or the stars at night in a black sky. Glory is often visual, and when we read the description of the New Jerusalem and the light that comes from God obviating the need for sun or moon, we are seeing yet another aspect of His glory. We also read about this in Genesis Chapter 1 verse 3.

Glory may be something that we can't see with the naked eye but which can be seen by the powerful Hubble telescope. Out there in space are galaxies, in numbers, sizes and distances beyond our understanding, making our beautiful Earth to be but a minute part of a pin prick by comparison Then there is the glory of grains of sand which can only be seen by using a very specialized microscope. When we see these things on-line we are amazed at the beauty and glory of God's creation.

The 'Unknown Christian' when writing on prayer suggested that we meditate on the glory and the grace of God before laying our petitions before Him. The writer added that we see the partial revelation of His glory in 'the surpassing glory of landscape, sunshine, sea and sky.' The writer continued, 'The telescope reveals His infinite glory. The microscope reveals His uttermost glory. Our dear Lord wants us to realise His infinite trustworthiness and unlimited power, so that we can approach

Him in simple faith and trust.' [128]

To me it is always a wonder to watch the first light appearing in the sky in midsummer, soon after 3:30 am. Moment by moment the light increases: it is unstoppable. As I look, from utter blackness bushes emerge, a wall, trees, and flowers. Daylight arrives; the glory and miracle of a new day.

THE 'COLOURS' OF GLORY

The Hebrew word 'doxa' which is translated as 'glory' in the Bible has the sense of brightness, splendour, magnificence, and majesty, distinction, or honour. It is sometimes said that a person has 'gone to Glory' meaning heaven. Strangely, the place under the stairs where I was taken to shelter during the war was called 'the glory-hole.'

It would appear from Ephesians Chapter 3 verses 14-17 that God's glory also contains the essence of His attributes. For instance, we read that there are riches of His glory which include power that will strengthen us, but in the Old Testament there is a word of warning in Isaiah Chapter 48 verse 11. God says that He will not give His glory to another. It is most unwise to boast, claiming glory and praise for ourselves.

---

[128] The Unknown Christian, 1986, p55

GLORY AND GRACE

Paul introduces the word 'glory' to describe the New Covenant of grace. He talks about the time when Moses came down from the mountain having been with God and receiving the Ten Commandments. The Israelites who were watching saw that his face was shining with glory. As this began to fade Moses covered his face with a veil, so that onlookers would not see the fading. Paul goes on to say that if the Old Covenant with the Law brought glory which faded, how much more glorious is the New Covenant through Jesus Christ which does not fade.[129]

HABAKKUK PROMISES

Finally, the prophet Habakkuk shows us a victorious end-time promise;

'For the earth will be filled with the knowledge of the glory of the Lord, as the waters cover the sea.'[130]

This time will surely come.

The glorious morning of sapphires and glory came to an end. It was time to finish in prayer and praise.

---

[129] 2 Corinthians 3:7-11
[130] Habakkuk 2:14

Prophetic Word

My dear children, I do indeed call on you to watch and pray.
Do not be disturbed, distracted or deviate from My ways by the things you hear. Only hear My voice, My still small voice. Do not be influenced by people, even people close to you, who would bring the enemy's voice to you. Be aware that he is as a roaring lion seeking whom he may devour; But the Lion of Judah stands with you. So keep close to Me and to each other. There is power in your unity in the Holy Spirit.
Remember this.

DAY 6

PEACE

'I am leaving you with a gift - peace of mind and heart.'
John 14:27a NLT
'You will keep in perfect peace all who trust in you, whose thoughts are fixed on you.' *Isaiah 26:3 NLT*

THE MORNING started like this,
'Lord I'm not sure where to go this morning. I have anxieties. You know.'
'Listen to Me My child. Hear My voice. I know all. I see all. Rest in Me.'
(The Scripture, 'In quietness and confidence shall be your strength'[131] comes to my mind.)
'Now you have the choice to believe My Word, or to sink into worry.'
'Lord I choose to lay it all down before you and to move on. You know everything and have all the answers.'

Once again I turned to the Word and looked at several verses from Psalm 112.

---

[131] Isaiah 30:15b NKJV

'Blessed is the man who fears the Lord.
Who finds great delight in his commands.
He will have no fear of bad news;
His heart is steadfast, trusting in the Lord,
His heart is secure; he will have no fear;
In the end he will look in triumph on his foes.'

After much worship and praise, my heart became steadfast and trusting and I felt able to ask;
'Lord is there another stone for me to find?'
'There are many My child. Now look for the very precious one called Peace.'

With that, I am once more on the Beach, walking, enjoying the lap of the waves, the warmth in the air, the sense of quiet joy and wellbeing. The Lord and I begin to talk again.
'What does this stone look like Lord?'
'Peace is a pure white stone - glorious in its whiteness: white because it is the absence of all darkness - no spots, no uncleanness - but white.'
'Lord, where is this stone? When I find it do I pick it up?'
Then the Lord surprised me.
'No, My child. Look - I give it to you, freely, for you to keep.'
There was no searching needed this time. It all happened so quickly and straight away I turned to receive the stone as it was put into my hand. It was soft to my touch, light emanating from it gently and I remembered His words, 'Peace I leave with you; my peace I give you. I do not give to you as the world gives. Do not let your heart be troubled and do not be afraid.'[132]

---

[132] John 14:27

I began to experience His wonderful peace. Life is so busy. To be busy and to have peace at the same time is rest. To be busy and not have peace is stress.
'Thank you Lord for Your wonderful gift.'

PEACE PERFECT PEACE

Peace is such a wonderful gift. Times of anxiety rob us of it. Times when God seems absent when we need Him. There are times when anxiety drives trust away, far away and as we look into the future our imagination sees a black and hopeless picture.

At these times we really do need a special word from God which will banish our imaginings and bring His truth to bear in the situation. There may be difficult times to go through and then we need to know that He really is with us. Fear is the great enemy of peace, and to get through to praising the Lord at these times will help drive it away. Here is another helpful acronym for 'fear:'

FALSE **E**VIDENCE **A**PPEARING **R**EAL

There is increasingly much to be fearful about these days, and we know that fear can paralyse. When it hits we must actively choose to turn to the Lord for His help and trust Him. 'Trust in the Lord with all your heart and lean not on your own understanding. In all your ways acknowledge him and he will make your paths straight.'[133]

---

[133] Proverbs 3:5-6

We are also often helped by sharing worries with trusted friends who can see through the situation clearly and give Godly advice. Trust! Make a decision to trust. And keep trusting! He is God Almighty. He has everything under His control and He is faithful. Here is a word He spoke to me recently,

'**My dear child, My dear children,**

Time is getting short and I exhort you to walk carefully in these days of wickedness. Do not take the world's road but seek that narrow path that leads to eternal life.

You do not know how many days are left before you, so treat each day as exceedingly precious. My hand is upon you, to steady you, lead you, support you, embrace you.

My love is upon you to uphold you, encourage you, envision you, comfort you.

So My dear children, walk in My ways, without hesitation. See the doors that I open before you, and enter my purposes for you. Do not be afraid but enter with confidence and with trust. Allow Me to lead you and even when the ground is unfamiliar and is beyond your comprehension; yet follow Me, for I go before you.'

As these thoughts fill my mind I am automatically led to His Word.

The Beach fades.

Peace

PEACE - Calmness - Tranquility - Trust

Isaiah gave this prophecy about Jesus Christ seven hundred years before His birth, not only giving the expectation of the Messiah's birth, but also describing His wonderful names;
'For to us a Child is born,
Unto us a Son is given.
And the government will be upon His shoulder.
And His name will be called.
Wonderful, Counsellor, Mighty God,
Everlasting Father, Prince of Peace.' [134]

Jesus Christ, the Prince of Peace is the source of our peace. When He is in our life, and He is our life, then His peace is a free gift to us. It is then that we realise the Lord is well able to help us in every situation, standing with us, giving us wisdom, changing things, or not changing things, but giving us strength and perseverance to bear them. The outcome is that our trust begins to grow; the grip of fear slackens and our perspective changes. We let God into the situation with His plans, and faith begins to replace unbelief. His grace is at work in our lives and

---

[134] Isaiah 9:6 NKJV

His perfect love is driving out our fear.[135] We begin to tackle the situation. Isaiah said that the government rests on Christ's shoulders. Let us place our burden on His broad shoulders; He will carry it.

Relationships can be the cause of much lack of peace. In many ways, life is made up of relationships and in them we can either have peace or stress. Do we need help in this area? Again the Bible has help. We are advised to seek peace and to pursue it in the Psalms (34:4). In an unforeseen difficult situation we are called to take the path which will restore or bring peace even if we seem to lose by it. Paul shares some practical advice when writing to the believers in Rome who were having problems with personal relationships:

- When others are happy, be happy with them if they are sad, share their sorrow.
- Live in harmony with each other.
- Don't try to act important, but enjoy the company of ordinary people. And don't think you know it all!
- Never pay back evil for evil to anyone. Do things in such a way that everyone can see you are honourable.
- Do your best to live in peace with everyone, as much as possible.
- Dear friends, never take revenge. Leave that to God.[136]

---

[135] 1 John 4:18
[136] Romans 12:15-19 NLT

Jesus made it very simple by saying, 'treat people the way that you want to be treated.'[137] Does this imply that we are at everyone's beck and call? Not really. It is a lifelong journey to have the wisdom to know when to say 'no' and when to say 'yes' to people, and how to say it and keep our boundaries in place.

Another issue that takes away peace is that of un-forgiveness. Harbouring un-forgiveness, sometimes over decades, often causes not only a deep lack of peace but can also produce illnesses. So many people say, 'But you don't know what I have had to suffer. I cannot forgive.' Well Jesus says we must. He says, 'If you forgive those who sin against you, your Heavenly Father will forgive you. But if you refuse to forgive others, your Father will not forgive your sins.'[138]

This makes it pretty clear. No matter what the circumstance, we must forgive. So how can we, when we feel we just can't? I believe this is where the grace of God comes in. If we genuinely want to but can't, the best thing is to confess this to Him in prayer. Be honest. Then if we are willing to be willing and say so, we can ask His help in the matter. We can make a firm decision to forgive in obedience, and He will in His time bring us to the place where we can forgive from the heart.

It will help to pray for the person, or persons, involved, no matter how we feel. Afterwards and in God's time comes not only peace, but answers to prayers that have been waiting in the wings. One of the ways that we know we have progressed in this matter is when we realise that we no longer want to tell our

---

[137] Matthew 7:12
[138] Matthew 6:14 NLT

sad story to others. The matter is closed.

At this time of writing, Christmas is approaching and I see stress overtaking so many people. Unrealistic expectations, overload of appointments on the calendar, family traditions or no family traditions, job loss, financial worries etc. all pile up in a heap. Peace is lost. Sadly it is a time when people will go into debt, when after the happy time of unwrapping presents comes the New Year difficulty of paying off the debt with added interest.

What is the answer? To all of these things, and more, Jesus Himself has and is the answer. He is the Prince of Peace and when we fully turn to him, He gives us wisdom to deal with the situation and will often use the good advice of friends. The prophet Isaiah gave some wonderful advice,
'You will keep him in perfect peace,
Whose mind is stayed on You
Because he trusts in You.' [139]
Trust is the key. When we can get to the place where we know we can trust God completely in whatever is worrying us, then we move into peace.

Billy Graham in his book 'Peace with God' quoted Browning, saying, 'The best is yet to be' and continued, 'This doesn't mean the Christian can never suffer defeat or experience low periods in his life. But it does mean that the Saviour goes with you no matter what the problem. The peace comes in the midst of problems and in spite of them.'[140]

---

[139] Isaiah 26:3 NKJV
[140] Graham, 1984, p30

Also there are times when we need to look at a problem and think whether or not we have unrealistic expectations. If so, once we dismiss them from the scene, we can relax and take peace. Sometimes we can be our own worst enemy and a good friend who can look at the problem and give an honest assessment even though it initially hurts, will prove to be a friend indeed.

HOW?

For those who have no relationship with God to start with, how do you initially get to this place of peace with God? Again, Dr. Graham, along with innumerable Christians, gives the simple answer:

- Believe that Jesus Christ is the Son of God and has died in your place to give you forgiveness.
- Repent of your sins which means not just saying sorry but determining with God's help to turn away from them.
- By faith ask God to be Lord and Saviour of your life.

Then peace will become a reality, as Paul said, 'Therefore since we have been made right in God's sight by faith, we have peace with God because of what Jesus Christ our Lord has done for us.'[141]

To have been 'made right' is a way of understanding the word 'justified' which is used in other translations.

---

[141] Romans 5:1 NLT

JUSTIFICATION

Through the inspiration of the Holy Spirit the Apostle Paul wrote, 'Therefore, since we have been justified through faith, we have peace with God through our Lord Jesus Christ.'[142]
To be justified means to be 'just -as-if we-had-never-sinned.'

This means that when God looks at us He sees us as if we had never sinned. How can this be possible? It is through our faith in Jesus Christ and His atoning sacrifice on the Cross. (Atonement is the act of providing reconciliation between God and man). We have been 'made right in God's sight.'

PEACE LIKE A RIVER

Isaiah wrote this regarding Jerusalem,
'Rejoice with Jerusalem and be glad for her, all you who love her;
Rejoice greatly with her all you who mourn over her.'
'For this is what the Lord says:
I will extend peace to her like a river,
and the wealth of nations like a flooding stream.'[143]

The situation in Jerusalem and Israel is far from peaceful at this time. The key indicator on the prophetic time-line is the fulfillment of the re-gathering of the Jewish nation into its own land. Despite constant wars, the time will come when peace will reign. The Prince of Peace will return.

---

[142] Romans 5:1a
[143] Isaiah 66:10 and 12a

Then I heard the Lord say,

'This river of peace flows strongly, is smooth, brings overwhelming peace wherever it flows, covers the jagged rocks and stones of anxiety and worry. My peace is like a river- because I see all and know all and in Me is all the wisdom needed and the power to overcome all things at all times.'

This peace of God that extends like a river will in His time flow over Jerusalem and the nations will know of it. We have His personal promise for ourselves also,

'Peace I leave with you; my peace I give you. I do not give to you as the world gives. Do not let your hearts be troubled and do not be afraid.'[144]

Why does Jesus say so much about peace? During His life on earth, He of all men had the most cause to be stressed, tired, discouraged and fearful, all of which can lead to a lack of peace. His time in the garden of Gethsemane just before being arrested is evidence of this, and the way He dealt with it can help us. He did what He always did when in great need, He went straight to His Father, and this time after a mighty spiritual battle He came through to peace.

None of us will ever face what He faced, but the things that try to rob us of peace are just as important to us and need to be dealt with. The Lord surely knows our needs and promises to give it to us. Today His peace is vital.

---

[144] John 14:27

I thanked God for such a lovely morning.
'We get there child don't we! I never fail you. In Me are all the riches of the treasures of heaven. This is one of My treasures for you; Peace, that passes understanding.'

I turned to a special blessing that the Lord gave to Moses for the people of Israel.

'The Lord bless you and keep you;
The Lord make His face shine upon you,
And be gracious to you;
The Lord lift up His countenance upon you,
And give you peace.'[145]

Surely this is a blessing for us also.
A quiet end to the day.

---

[145] Numbers 6:23-26

Prophetic Word

My dear child,
If you wait on Me, you will find that My time is the perfect time and all will work together for good. You are learning to wait for My Holy Spirit to lead you. In this waiting time you will find that you have My peace, and worry cannot find entrance, and lead you to pre-empting My will.
So continue to learn and lean on Me and not your own understanding, and then My will and your desires will find fruition and be accomplished.
Peace is the outcome of trust.

Victory

DAY 7

VICTORY

'Better a patient man than a warrior, a man who controls his temper than one who takes a city.'   *Proverbs 16:32*
'But thanks be to God! He gives us the victory through our Lord Jesus Christ.'   *1 Corinthians 15:57*

A NEW DAY, and this is my morning reading,
'All men are like grass,
And all their glory is like the flowers of the field.
The grass withers and the flowers fall,
Because the breath of the Lord blows on them.
Surely the people are grass.
The grass withers and the flowers fall, but the word of our God stands forever.'[146]

    Straightaway, without any thought or conversation, I am back on the Beach! It is a very different beach today. There is a storm coming. The sky is dark. Rolling black and dark purple clouds are making for the shore. The wind is getting up. It looks most ominous and it is very unlike previous visits. Then the Lord and I begin to talk.

---

[146] Isaiah 40 6-8

'What is happening Lord?'
'It is not a problem My child. Walk on. I am with you.'
'There is rain and wind Lord. Will I be able see another precious stone now amongst the pebbles?'
'It is there My child. Walk on. You will prevail.'
I crouch down, and take cover against the weather. The storm is gale-force now.
'Speak out child and take authority over it, don't bow before it.'
And say? Then I knew what to say and how to take authority. It was a case of commanding it to go in the name of the Lord Jesus Christ.
'Storm cease and go in the name of the Lord Jesus Christ!'
In a matter of moments the rain stops, the dark clouds scurry away and disperse, the sun is out - all is fresh, clean, and bright. Then it was time to ask the Lord about today's jewel.
'Which stone do You want me to look for Lord? I have no idea.'
'My child, there are lots to choose from; but for now, look for the victory stone.'
'Victory? What does this stone look like?'
'This jewel has many colours - you will see black streaks, yellow parts, blue streaks and from it, red will seep out covering the other colours.'
I asked the reason for this.
'There are many aspects to warfare. The yellow is the poison, the poison of tongues; the dark blue is the dark of the storm blotting out the light of the sun, the black streaks are the streaks of the evil one, lies and deception attempting to cover the stone. But the red is the blood of Jesus which oozes out and covers the whole stone. Watch. The stone will be transformed.'
I walk on and find the multi-coloured stone, recognizing it by the colours, the black and yellow, with blue

patches and then the strange effect of redness coming out of it and covering the other colours. For some reason, which I cannot grasp, it has been difficult to walk over the sand towards the stone which I can now see. As I am considering how to pick it up and bend down towards it, there is a total change in its appearance.
'Lord, it is blazing with light. I can pick it up now and the light transforms the ground around me. I can walk easily on the sand. The stone lights the way. It is protective.'
'So think about this child. The blood of Jesus transforms, brings victory, and brings light. My Son gave His life for this victory. It is assured. So remember, in the storm look for the victory. It is always there. There is no need to be apprehensive or fear at this morning's stone. It is all in My hand, even as it is in your hand. Walk on. The victory is sweet and pleasant and delightful. We will laugh together in it and be joyful.

Once again I am keen to get into the Word of God.

Victory

ONE THING that the new Christian quickly learns is that we are 'born again' on to a battlefield. We have an enemy who will constantly and consistently attempt to overcome us. Jesus said when describing Satan, 'he comes only to steal and kill and destroy; I have come that they might have life and have it to the full."[147] However, we also learn that the Lord has provided all we need to remain safe in Him and have the victory.

When we think of victory our first question is, who or what are we fighting? There is a quick answer in Ephesians 6 verse 12,

'For our struggle is not against flesh and blood, but against the rulers, against the authorities, against the powers of this dark world and against the spiritual forces of evil in the heavenly realms.'

The problem comes when we think that we are fighting flesh and blood. We think that people are the problem and we are not discerning that we are in a spiritual war; it is the agents of Satan that are influencing the people and situations. Then, because we are not dealing with the root of the problem, it becomes almost impossible to solve or overcome.

We really need to seek the Lord and His Word, asking

---

[147] John 10:10

for wisdom and revelation on how to pray. Jesus said that the Holy Spirit would lead us into all truth, so we need His help. We are blessed if we have praying friends who will seek God and pray with authority for and with us.

During the Second World War the warfare was both physical and spiritual. Faithful Christian intercessors were given words of Scripture, prophecies, pictures, or visions during prayer times. These were keys to bringing physical victory in battles. Rees Howells and his group of intercessors in South Wales took part in such spiritual battles behind the scenes, which brought many unexpected victories. King George V1 himself called for two national days of prayer in 1940, both of which came at times of imminent disaster.

Air Chief Marshall Sir Hugh Dowding, Commander-in-Chief of Fighter Command, was asked at this time about his plans to defeat the overwhelming number of the German Air Force. He replied: 'I believe in God. And there is radar.'[148] After the war, Lord Dowding said this, 'Even during the battle one realised from day to day how much external support was coming in. At the end of the battle one had the sort of feeling that there had been some special Divine intervention to alter some sequence of events which would otherwise have occurred.'[149]

This particular battle was crucial in the battle for Britain on September 15, 1940. The situation looked hopeless as German squadrons filled British air space.[i] For Lord Dowding,

---

[148] Russell, K. 2014
[149] Grubb, N. 2014 p178

prayer was the number one priority with radar a close second, and this viewpoint was emphasized in a certain scene in the film, 'Battle of Britain.'

What are our priorities when we hit difficult situations and on what grounds can we expect to be victorious? Paul wrote this to the Church in Ephesus;

'I pray that you will begin to understand the incredible greatness of his power for us who believe him. This is the same mighty power that raised Christ from the dead and seated him in the place of honour at God's right hand in the heavenly realms.'[150] We stand our ground on the power of the victory that Christ has already won at the Cross. As the Apostle John said, 'The One who is in you is greater than the one who is in the world'[151]

What is our spiritual equivalent of radar and modern weaponry? Again the answer found in the Scriptures at the end of Paul's letter to the Ephesians, where we read of the armour and the weapon that God has supplied for us.

'A final word: be strong with the Lord's mighty power. Put on all of God's armour so that you will be able to stand firm against all the strategies and tricks of the Devil. For we are not fighting against people made of flesh and blood, but against the evil rulers and authorities of the unseen world, against those mighty powers of darkness who rule this world, and against wicked spirits in the heavenly realms.

Use every piece of God's armour to resist the enemy in the time of evil, so that after the battle you will still be standing

---

[150] Ephesians 1:19-20 NLT
[151] 1 John 4:4b

firm. Stand your ground, putting on the sturdy belt of truth and the body armour of God's righteousness. For shoes, put on the peace that comes from the Good News, so that you will be fully prepared. In every battle you will need faith as your shield to stop the fiery arrows aimed at you by Satan.

Put on salvation as your helmet, and take the sword of the Spirit, which is the word of God. Pray at all times and on every occasion in the power of the Holy Spirit. Stay alert and be persistent in your prayers for all Christians everywhere.'[152]

Spiritual warfare requires the spiritual weapons that are provided for us; then we also have head to foot protection. Our supreme weapon, His Word, is described as 'living, active and sharper than any double- edged sword.'[153] This is why we need to know our Bible. Of course, Jesus is the Word. It is His voice speaking.

Paul must have pondered much on the armour of the Roman soldiers especially when he was chained to them during his times of imprisonment. The Holy Spirit was then able to give him revelation about spiritual armour and the weapons provided for believers. It surely revolutionised his prayer time whilst in prison, and became a vital teaching for all the Churches.

Some people may 'pray the armour on' day by day; others believe that by remaining faithfully 'in Christ' daily, they already have their armour on. We need a day by day walk of obedience, with time spent in His presence and in the Word.

---

[152] Ephesians 6:10-18 NLT
[153] Hebrews 4:12

LEARNING FROM HISTORY?

We can learn a lot about spiritual warfare through reading about the physical battles Israel had in the Old Testament. It is always useful to realise that many Old Testament events help us to understand their spiritual counterparts in the New Testament. We see how God led the Israelites into battle, gave them warnings, and brought them victories which were outrageously impossible and won by illogical strategies.

Conversely, when they were in disobedience they suffered defeat. For instance the battle for Jericho was won by marching around the city seven times silently until the last moment, then blowing trumpets and shouting.[154] Or was it? Would these actions really cause the magnificent walls of Jericho to fall down and the city be taken? It had to be a supernatural move of God, perfectly timed, alongside the total obedience of the people. And then came the shout of faith and down came the walls!

However, their next battle was altogether a different matter. Unbeknown to Joshua, one of the men had seen a beautiful cloak during the Jericho battle and had taken it home with bars of silver and gold, disregarding God's warning about such behavior;

'The city and all that is in it are to be devoted to the Lord…But keep away from the devoted things, so that you will not bring about your own destruction by taking any of them. Otherwise you will make the camp of Israel liable to destruction and bring

---

[154] Joshua 6:3-4

trouble on it. All the silver and gold and the articles of bronze and iron are sacred to the Lord and must go into his treasury.'[155]

Consequently this next battle to take the city of Ai ended in disaster. The men sent to spy out the situation had thought it would be a walkover. They advised Joshua to take only a group of three thousand warriors rather than the whole company. The result was total defeat, not because of the numbers involved but because of the previous disobedience of that one man in the battle for Jericho. A severe judgement followed.

This man had been identified as the culprit through the drawing of lots and all Israel had been watching. Those who had lost fathers, brothers, husbands and sons now knew who was to blame and Achan was forced to confess. He had buried all the items in his tent, so Joshua sent men to investigate and they returned with all the treasures. His family would have known all about it and had kept quiet. The day ended in catastrophic retribution - death for them all.[156]

Can we learn anything from these stories that happened so long ago, lessons that would help us today in spiritual warfare? Firstly, we need to recognise or discern when it is matter of spiritual warfare and not as we think, just 'circumstances.' Then we ally ourselves with Jesus, knowing that at the Cross, Satan was defeated. We take our stand in Christ. He had cried, 'It is finished,'[157] just before He died and

---

[155] Joshua 6:17-19
[156] Joshua 7:25
[157] John 19:30

from the tense of the word used, (Greek tetelestai) it means that the victory over Satan was complete once and for all, not needing to be repeated. It was absolute and the ensuing atonement perfectly perfect and completely complete.

However we can learn from Achan's sin that we need to make sure we don't have 'accursed' objects in our homes, things that belong to false religions or the occult.

'Do not bring a detestable thing into your house, or you like it will be set apart for destruction. Utterly abhor and detest it, for it is set apart for destruction.'[158]

As Christians why would we want to give house-room to something that was set apart for destruction?[159] It is easy to bring a memento back from holiday, not realizing its spiritual significance. My husband and I thought we had cleared our house of all such things but one year we bought a beautiful rug when on holiday, which some time later we realised was a prayer rug of another faith. Although to us it looked so beautiful, it had to go in obedience to the Lord.

Another time we brought back with us a stone model of a man's head from Africa. After a while we began to be most uneasy and realised that the Holy Spirit was speaking to both of us about it. He knew things that we did not about its origins and as our Helper; He was leading us into all truth. Some will dismiss this advice as being excessive but we have found that when the Lord reveals a truth to us and a course of action is needed, the best and only thing to do is to be obedient. The

---

[158] Deuteronomy 7:26
[159] ibid

stone head was smashed in the garden and relegated to the bin.

In many ways, there are spiritual pointers found in the two battles mentioned. If we have been involved in previous battles we can be encouraged by the past victories but not to expect the next one to go along the same lines. For example, many years after Joshua's death, Jehoshaphat, the King of Judah, had news of an overwhelmingly vast enemy army approaching Jerusalem. Everyone was terrified and the whole population gathered together to seek God, even the small children and mothers with babes in arms. God spoke to them all through a prophet called Jahaziel,
'Do not be afraid or discouraged because of this vast army. For the battle is not yours but God's…You will not have to fight this battle. Take your positions; stand firm and see the deliverance the Lord will give you, O Judah and Jerusalem. Do not be afraid; do not be discouraged. Go out to face them tomorrow, and the Lord will be with you.' [160]

Immediately they were all on their faces before God, worshipping and the next day the army set out to face the foe. But Jehoshaphat had, like Joshua years before, been given a strategy. A praising choir was to lead the army into battle singing, 'Give thanks to the Lord, for His loving kindness is everlasting.' Can we imagine a modern day army being led to war by the Church choir? Nevertheless, when Jehoshaphat's men reached the battlefield an amazing sight met their eyes. It was littered with dead bodies. Not one living enemy soldier remained. What had happened? Of the three armies that had

---

[160] 2 Chronicles 20:15b,17

come to fight against Israel, two of them had joined forces against the other one and killed them all. Having finished the slaughter they then turned against each other so that not one survived.[161]

There was so much spoil to take that it took Jehoshaphat's men three days to carry it all back to their camp. The steps into victory were: desperate prayer to the Lord, His promise of success, His strategy, their obedience and then His control of the situation. The people were obedient, and victory ensued. For us the strategy given by the Holy Spirit is vital, and it may be that a simple plan will help build up our faith. We can find relevant scriptures and read them daily, which will lead into a definite prayer of faith.

We know of a family that was most upset as their young child was being bullied and lied about by another family. The parents sought God recognizing that this was not a case of 'flesh and blood' but part of a spiritual battle. They received from the Lord words from 2 Chronicles as noted above. They knew that they just had to continue to rely on the Lord, love and bless the people concerned and wait for God to act. Suddenly and unexpectedly the said family moved very quickly out of the area and the problem was solved. Again it was a case of having spiritual discernment regarding the reason for the attack, seeking the Lord and obeying His Word.

Pastor Frankie Dean-Deliu wrote the following regarding prayer; 'If you desire something from God, use the key that He has given you, which is prayer, to gain access to the

---

[161] 2 Chronicles 20:22-23

throne room of the King of kings and the Lord of lords. And then use your faith, which is your unwavering belief, and trust God's word to unlock the door to your blessings! See how simple it is? Whenever you pray, believe that God will do what He says he will do, pray in faith, pray the Word, and don't give the matter another thought.'[162]

Finally– PRAISE – When we enter into praising God, we find it to be a major factor in victory over Satan. We are submitting ourselves to God declaring His power and omnipotence, worshipping Him, drawing near to Him and He is drawing near to us. As James wrote, the devil then flees from us.[163] Worship invites victory.

THE WAY UP IS THE WAY DOWN

When a group of young Christians asked a certain well known Bible teacher, Lance Lambert,[164] what was the secret of living the Christian life, his reply was, 'Learn how to die.' Dying to self is something we don't like! Our pride and self-will rise up so easily. We justify ourselves mentally and vocally, but if we will put our trust in Christ, He will bring the victory to us.

---

[162] Dean-Deliu, 2011, p15
[163] James 4:7-8
[164] Lance went to be with the Lord on May 10th 2015.

STICKS AND STONES

Many believers, if not most, experience times when lies have been spread about them. You could almost say it is 'par for the course,' and running around trying to explain the truth and put things right is not always the best way to get the victory. Often, the better way is to leave it to the Lord Himself to bring out the whole truth His way.

Trusting Him to clear our name will eventually bring vindication, and He surely will in His time. But even if He doesn't in our lifetime, we know that He knows the truth about the situation and we have peace that we are righteous in His sight and not under His condemnation.

There is the story of Margaret Barber who went to China as a missionary. Out of jealousy, lies were spread about her and she had to return to England. She never vindicated herself and eventually after encouragement from a wise Bishop, she returned to China, relying entirely on the Lord for provision and direction

A group of young Chinese men and women began to meet with her, learning so much from this quiet Godly woman who taught them truth from the Word. One of them was the man who became known as Watchman Nee. He later proved to be a major influence in the Chinese Church, teaching and discipling the believers so thoroughly that they were able stand in the days of persecution during the years of Communism. His writings, for example 'The Spiritual Man,' are sought by believers today. He often mentioned Margaret Barber, the English lady who taught him so much. So be patient and trust

Him. He will vindicate His children.

Interestingly, God allows many difficult and testing situations to come our way and at these times this word in Romans Chapter 8:28 is one to take to heart,

'And we know that He causes all things to work together for good to those who love God, to those who are called according to His purpose.'

Yes, we need to work through the situation, yet be aware that God is working it through also.[165] Many lies and distortions were aimed at Jesus and He never justified Himself. There was the time when He was publicly denounced as an impostor because everyone knew that the Messiah was prophesied to come from Bethlehem and this man Jesus came from Nazareth —so they believed. What a perfect opportunity for Jesus to explain that actually His birthplace was Bethlehem. That would have settled the debate and vindicated Himself. But He did not say a word, and eventually everybody went home. He refused to justify Himself.

Oswald Chambers writing in 'The Place of Help'[166] reflected this problem saying that Jesus Christ can afford to be misunderstood but we cannot. He went on to say that our weakness lies in our always wanting to vindicate ourselves.

---

[165] Genesis 18:25b
[166] Chambers, 1989

PETER'S ADVICE

The Apostle Peter who in his early years with Christ used to speak first and think afterwards, became a source of great wisdom and maturity in later life. We see this in the two letters that we have access to in the New Testament. He wrote that, as we know Jesus better, his divine power gives us everything we need for living a godly life.[167] This ex-fisherman, now a changed man, had already proved the validity of this Holy Spirit inspired statement throughout the years in his own life. These words also encourage us, and as we look back, we recognize how we too have been changed by His love.

At this point the Lord spoke to me again,

'Be encouraged child as you read of victories. Now you see My child, on the Beach it was cold, wet and windy with little or no sun. The stone of victory transformed all this. Victory always does. My Word brings victory. It is the two-edged sword to speak into these situations. With My Word comes faith. You have faith to believe what I say. My grace is working for you. It is My gift. My will is thereby accomplished.'

Praise and worship then flowed and my morning ended.

---

[167] 2 Peter 1:3-5a NLT

Isaiah 41:10

'Do not fear for I am with you.
Do not be dismayed, for I am your God.
I will strengthen you and help you.
I will uphold you with My righteous right hand.'

Faith

DAY 8

FAITH

'Faith is taking the first step even when you don't see the whole staircase.' *Martin Luther King Jnr.*
'So faith comes from hearing the message, and the message is heard through the Word of Christ.' *Romans 10:17*
'Now faith is being sure of what we hope for and certain of what we do not see.' *Hebrews 11:1*
'Faith is the deliberate confidence in the character of God, whose ways you may not understand at the time.' *Oswald Chambers*

AFTER PRAISE IT SEEMED that today would be in some way unlike the previous days. I had been listening to a modern praise song which encourages us to believe that despite our difficulties, a way through would be made clear for us by God. This led me to say,
'Lord I praise You. I look to the new thing you will do today,' and it was good to hear Him reply,
'Good morning My child. Now hear My voice.'
So I waited and asked the Holy Spirit to help me.
In a moment I was there once more: the same Beach, but it was looking different today, certainly not the storm of yesterday, but not like other days either. So I kept walking.
Oh! I see a greenish flashing light on the sand.
When I approached it I see it was an enormous stone, the

surface was flat and big enough to stand on. As I step on to it, the stone becomes a vast pavement, large enough to walk on.

'I can't pick this up Lord. It is huge. It is flashing with light, exquisite!'

'So walk on it and look.'

It is breathtaking. I have never seen anything like this before. I walk on it. I can look down into it. There are different shades of green, and blue, a liquid and yet a solid sea, like an emerald, but vast, transparent, beautiful. Now as I look up, it stretches as far as the eye can see, in every direction. It is like walking on water, but solid water. I continue to walk, enjoying the fascinating moving colours of blues and greens beneath my feet. Then the Lord began to speak,

'Will you walk on water with Me child?'

'Yes Lord. This is beautiful.'

Then I understand the meaning of this vast pavement.

'Now I see! This is faith!'

'Yes - walking on faith. Your first thought was that this is such an experience, and this is true; faith and experience- experience and faith; walking in and on faith. It has no end and yes it is beautiful; faith in and on Me at all times, in all ways; the walk which is beautiful, firm to your feet, safe. Faith is your normal ordinary place to walk; the everyday way to walk. It stretches in all directions and wherever you need to go, you will walk on faith. It holds you up and it is beautiful.'

I was overwhelmed. For some time I kept walking on this incredibly beautiful pavement. But now the vision had gone and I was hungry to get into the Word on faith. But en route to faith I was led to Psalm 139,

'O Lord You have searched me and you know me,
You know when I sit and when I rise;
You perceive my thoughts from afar.
You discern my going out and my lying down;
You are familiar with all my ways.
Before a word is on my tongue,
You know it completely, O Lord.'[168]

As always, I know that these scriptures echo my thoughts and His truths. This leads me to a time of praise.

---

[168] Psalm 139:1-4

Faith

MANY PEOPLE seem to get discouraged about faith, worrying that they don't have faith, or haven't got enough, or what is faith anyway? Faith is certainly something to experience. We all understand simple everyday faith, as most of life involves using faith from trusting a chair to hold us to expecting the sun to rise every morning. There are so many commonplace things that we trust in and have faith in; things that don't let us down. So what about spiritual faith?

When we are very young children, we find it easy to believe in God, when we are told about Him and hear stories of Jesus. We know that when we talk to him, He hears and loves us. As small children we have trusting natures. Maybe this is why Jesus said we need to become as little children to enter the kingdom of God.

Later our experience of life-changing faith comes when we really hear the Gospel. The truth of it 'speaks' to us, becomes real to us, and afterwards when we consider what has happened we realise that faith was given to us as a gift, and it was not a difficult process at all. At that moment of hearing, of *really hearing,* the Holy Spirit caused faith to erupt in us. Things like the need for repentance and forgiveness, and the awareness of what Christ has done for us became real. We became new people - born again.

As we walk through life, faith becomes the vital ingredient in our maturing as a believer. We learn that there are ways of increasing and building up our faith. The Lord allows many challenging situations to come our way, and our desire to both please Him and come through difficulties means that faith in God and the knowledge of His love and faithfulness towards us are paramount.

One of the ways we learn about our God in whom we trust is to find out what He says, what He does, what are His plans for us, how will He help us and what happens if...? As we study His Word we find Him speaking into all these situations. Like students who increase in knowledge through study, so we increase our faith through the study of the One whom we serve, and our study book is the Bible. With the help of the Holy Spirit, our relationship grows, as does our faith.

TOO OLD?

Abraham trusted and believed when God spoke and promised him a son. How his faith was tested as the years went by! Both he and Sarah were now well past the age of childbearing, he being one hundred and Sarah ninety, and still no child. Yet Isaac-meaning 'laughter', was eventually born and God's covenant promise to Abraham was fulfilled. His name would always remind Sarah of the time when the Lord had given Abraham the promise of a son, and she had laughed incredulously.[169] Isaac's descendants would be as numerous as

---

[169] Genesis 18:9-15

the stars in the sky or sand on the shore and Abraham would be the father of a great nation.[170]

WALKING ON WATER

One of the most interesting faith events in the New Testament took place on the Sea of Galilee. The disciples were crossing the lake and battling against a storm. Jesus had stayed behind on the land to have time with His Father. As they fought the contrary wind, they saw Jesus walking towards them on the water. They were terrified, thinking it was a ghost, but Jesus spoke and told them not to be afraid. Then the still scared but impetuous Peter called out and said, 'Lord if it's You then command me to come to You on the water,' and Jesus said, 'Come!'[171]

I suspect that before Peter knew what he was doing he was out of the boat and walking on the water. All the time that he was hearing Jesus' voice saying 'Come!' and looking at Jesus, he walked, as Jesus walked. He surely experienced enough faith to take those first steps. A gift of faith! How did it come? Peter asked. Jesus said, 'Come'. Peter believed - and did the impossible.

Yet Peter began to sink when he looked at the waves and took his eyes off Jesus. Many times Jesus will encourage us to do what seems to us 'outrageous' things, believing Him for the impossible, and we sometimes call this 'walking on water.' Our faith is put to the test and we find that it holds. The key is in

---

[170] Genesis 17, 18:1-5, 21:1-7
[171] Matthew 14:28

hearing Him speak. We realise that as Jesus Himself said, 'My sheep hear My voice.'[172] We can expect Him to speak to us.

When we get into the Word, we start to read more about faith, for example; 'Now faith is being sure of what we hope for and certain of what we do not see.'[173]
Or as the NLT reads; 'Faith is the confidence that what we hope for will actually happen; it gives us assurance about things we cannot see.' Allowing His Word to sink deep into our hearts brings faith.

WHEN GOD SAYS 'YES'

There are times when in prayer, we hear the Lord say 'yes' to our request, either through His word or when He speaks directly to our spirit. It is then that we have this complete assurance and conviction that what we have asked for is already is ours, although it has not yet materialised.

Sometimes He may suddenly show us a picture in our 'mind's eye' of something we have been praying about: we 'know that we know' that the Lord is answering our prayer. This is faith. Then there are the wonderful times when we 'accidentally' come across some words of Scripture that exactly speak into the situation. We call it a 'rhema word.' It is God's voice directly to us. What we have asked for was already on God's heart, and we have just partnered with Him in the matter.

When a child asks for a bike for Christmas and his Dad

---

[172] John 10:27
[173] Hebrews 11:1

says 'yes,' the child knows he has that bike for sure. He is not slow in telling his friends all about his new bike, weeks before it arrives. He has faith and trusts his father. He trusts because he knows his Dad keeps his word. If we don't spend time each day delighting in the Bible and talking with our God and Father, then we won't be in a strong position to exercise faith, especially when the troubles come. Neither will we know how to pray and receive answers.

We often think that we haven't enough faith. At these times it is good to remember that Jesus said we only need faith the size of a mustard seed to initiate great deeds and nothing will be impossible to us.[174] Paul further wrote this to the church in Rome, 'So then faith comes by hearing, and hearing by the Word of God.'[175]

It often happens like this; we read the Word of God and something there 'speaks' to us. We may have read that Scripture a thousand times, but this time, it almost seems to leap off the page. Then we know it is the Lord speaking, and faith is born. We have our answer. Then we need to hold it fast. It may be a word of encouragement which is so needed, or the answer to a question you have and you know God is saying 'yes' or 'no'.

Whatever the situation, knowing His voice through the Word brings help and confirmation. Having a constant habit of reading and studying the Scriptures is one of the main ways of hearing God speak to us, and when we hear Him speak, then faith is born in us, and our fellowship with God is refreshed.

---

[174] Matthew 17:20
[175] Romans 10:17

The Apostle Paul says these things about faith:
- that we walk by faith and not by sight,
  2 Corinthians 5:7
- that he lives by faith in the Son of God,
  Galatians 2:20
- that we are saved and justified by faith.
  Romans 3:28

This last statement was instrumental in the emerging of the Reformation. It so happened that Martin Luther read this, 'For it is by grace you have been saved, through faith - and this not from yourselves, it is the gift of God-not by works, so that no- one can boast.'[176] He realised and understood the truth of this statement; salvation is a gift; no one can earn it or pay for it in any way. It is God's grace, freely offered, and accepted through faith

THE FAITH OF THE FIVE

Through their faith the following five women each received what they needed from Jesus;
DELIVERANCE: For her demonized daughter.

This Gentile woman had heard of Jesus' miracles and when He came to her town, she pleaded with Him to heal her demonized daughter. The ensuing conversation proved her belief in Him and Christ commended her for her faith. The daughter was

---

[176] Ephesians 2:8-9

healed and delivered immediately.[177]

FORGIVENESS: This woman was described as a 'sinner,' probably a prostitute.

Here is the lovely story of the woman who wept over Jesus' feet. Jesus was dining with Simon the Pharisee and she entered weeping, and began to kiss His feet, anointing them with perfume. Simon was outraged that Jesus would allow this woman to touch Him. How did Jesus react? He spoke to Simon by name and told him a story.

There were two men who were in dire straits, being unable to pay off their debts and thus being in danger of imprisonment or slavery. The money lender was compassionate and forgave them both.

"Who would love him more," asked Jesus, "he one who had owed a little or the one who owed ten times as much?" Simon of course knew the answer, and Jesus then gently pointed out the lack of good manners in Simon's hospitality; no water had been provided for His feet, the kiss of welcome and the oil of anointing, were lacking, all of which would have been common courtesies at that time. These things the woman had provided in her own outstanding way. Jesus continued,

'Therefore I tell you, her many sins have been forgiven-for she loved much. But he who has been forgiven little loves little". Then Jesus said to her, "Your sins are forgiven." and continued, 'Your faith has saved you; go in peace.'"[178]

---

[177] Matthew 15:21-28
[178] Luke 7:36-50

HEALING: This woman was bent double.

She had not been able to straighten up for eighteen years, an illness caused by an evil spirit. Jesus had compassion on her when He saw her in the Synagogue and when He laid His hands on her, she immediately stood upright. How she praised and gave God the glory. She was free. Again there was official opposition. It was the Sabbath and this miracle should have been done on one of the other six days![179]

NEW LIFE AND REVIVAL: Jesus met this Samaritan woman by the town well.

It was midday and hot. Jesus was tired and thirsty and asked the woman to draw water for Him. Now this was an extraordinary situation. Jews did not speak to or have anything to do with Samaritans, and especially with a woman. The division between them went back to 722BC when the Assyrians had captured the northern kingdom of Israel and carried off many of the Jews to Assyria. Their place was taken by Gentiles, brought in by the Assyrians to resettle the land.

These foreigners brought with them their pagan idol worship and it was not long before the Jews were intermarrying with them and adopting idol worship. Thus there was much mixture in the Samaritan's worship. However Jesus had deliberately opted to travel through Samaria on His way to Galilee and His purpose became clear as they talked. A conversation developed between them as she asked Him

---

[179] Luke 13:12-16

questions, and when the topic of worship came up Jesus began to talk about 'living water' and eternal life.

She told Him that the Messiah was coming who would explain all these things; whereupon Jesus said that He was the Messiah. He had already shown her that He knew of her past lifestyle with five husbands and her present domestic situation of living with a sixth, who was not her husband. However, this one meeting with the Lord convinced and convicted her. She believed in Him and went back to tell the men in the town. The outcome was a major turning to Christ in this Samaritan town, Sychar. The people asked Jesus to stay and this He did, teaching and preaching to them for two days. Many of them believed and a revival was born.[180]

HEALING FROM 'AN ISSUE OF BLOOD': This woman was desperate.

She had been ill with constant bleeding for twelve years and had spent all her money on doctors but without success. Not only was this a debilitating illness but it also marked her as unclean religiously. Jesus was already on His way to heal the dying twelve year old daughter of a man called Jairus, when this woman crept up and in faith touched the hem of His garment. Immediately she knew she was healed.

The crowd was pushing and shoving around Jesus and the disciples at this point, but He knew that someone had touched Him with that special touch of faith. 'Who touched Me?' He asked. Of course she then admitted it, telling everyone nearby that she was healed. Jesus looked at her, saying,

---

[180] John 4:5-42

'Daughter your faith has made you well; go in peace.'[181]

Is Jesus any different today? I am always touched by this last miracle having been totally healed of a similar complaint myself many years ago, so that the planned hysterectomy operation was cancelled. Likewise I also knew immediately when I was healed.

HEBREWS CHAPTER 11 - THE PEOPLE OF FAITH

This weighty Chapter is all about Old Testament people of faith and there is quite a list, but it starts off with the following definition of faith;
'What is faith? It is the confident assurance that what we hope for is going to happen. It is the evidence of things we cannot yet see. God gave approval to people in days of old because of their faith. By faith we understand that the entire universe was formed at God's command, that what we now see did not come from anything that can be seen.'[182]

Interestingly the writer of Hebrews says that all the people mentioned died without receiving the promises but they had seen them and knew that they would come.[183]

---

[181] Luke 8:43-48
[182] Hebrews 11:1-3 NLT
[183] Hebrews 11:13

RECOGNIZING FAITH

If we want to grow in our faith it is so important for us to make reading, studying and meditating in the Word our lifestyle. If faith comes by hearing the Word of God then we need to have more than a passing acquaintance with it

Some years ago we learned the following from Kevin Duffy, a Bible teacher in South Africa:

Doubt despairs, complains and is sad.
Faith rejoices gives thanks and is glad.
Faith always simplifies --and it's easy
Doubt always complicates ---and it's hard.
Faith comes by hearing the answer.
Doubt comes by talking the problem.

Sometimes we substitute presumption for faith. We need to know the difference because one leads to victory and the other leads to disappointment and doubt. Presumption is twinned with assumption and both are built on the foundation of our own hopeful wishes. By contrast the Bible talks about a 'living' or 'lively' hope which is a hope built on Jesus Christ and the veracity of God's Word and His character.[184] We can read about this kind of hope in David's Psalms.

We may assume something, hoping it will come about, but 'without faith' it says in Hebrews 11 'it is impossible to please God, because when we come to God we must believe that He is and that He rewards those who persevere in seeking

---

[184] 1 Peter 1:3

Him.'[185] Faith means that we know that we know. We know that our request has been granted, and recognize the faithfulness of God. Presumption is on a different level: we just have a vain hope.

There are many times when we just take the Word of God as it stands, believing utterly in the truth of it and the faithfulness of God, and in so doing we exercise faith. This tiny seed of faith, God accepts, and the Word becomes true so that 'hope does not disappoint us.'[186] God is God!

Faith is evident all through the New Testament. Jesus was always looking for it in people who came to Him. He cherished the tiniest amount of faith in a person, and still does today.

A DISRUPTED FUNERAL

We find that whenever Jesus healed, faith was involved somewhere, either in the person being healed or in the one who brought the sick person to Him.

One day He came upon a large crowd weeping and mourning as a coffin was being carried to the burial. A young man, the only son of a widow had died, and as Jesus watched He was filled with compassion. The dead son was the widow's only means of support and she was possibly facing becoming a beggar. Not only that, but this her beloved boy was dead.

Here, the only one with faith would have been Jesus

---

[185] Hebrews 11:6
[186] Romans 5:5

Himself as there is no record of the widow appealing to Him. We can imagine the fear as well as delight and thanksgiving when at Jesus' command the young man sat up and began to speak. I wonder what he said?

DON'T LET GO!

A friend of ours was in great distress with a back complaint that had troubled her for many years. She had tried all the usual medical ways and doubted it would ever be healed. However, she was happy to be prayed for. Her husband also advised it. So we anointed her with oil and we prayed. We were amazed and somewhat alarmed as she began to twist and turn in many different positions. After a time she stopped, smiled and said that all pain had gone.

She knew she was completely healed. How we praised God! In the days that followed she could do all the things that she had not been able to do before, like opening the up-and-over garage door. A month or so later a neighbour called. He was upset because he was having a problem gardening and needed help. 'I hope he's not going to ask me,' she thought. 'He knows I've got a bad back.' Immediately her back pain came back and it was not until she sought God and repented of that thought that it left. We must hold on in faith to the healing that God gives us, as we have an enemy who will attempt to wrest it from us.

FINALLY

The Apostle Paul taught that even if we had great faith unless we were governed by love, our faith would not count for much.

- 1 Corinthians 13:2 - If I have a faith that can remove mountains, but have not love, I am nothing
- Romans 14:1 - Accept the one who is weak in faith but not for the purpose of passing judgement on his opinions.
- 1Corinthians 13:13 - And now these three remain: faith, hope and love. But the greatest of these is love.

This wonderful gift of faith that we are given is the vital ingredient in all our lives. We don't have to look for it, but when we need it, we know that the Lord provides.

'The righteous will live by faith' wrote Paul,[187] or as another translation reads, 'The man who is righteous by faith shall live.' Whichever way we look at it - faith in Jesus Christ, who loves us is the mainstay of our life. Prayer closed this time.

---

[187] Romans 1:17

Prophetic word

My dear children,

Have you noticed how the days are fleeing? And have you noticed how the world's events are rushing by? Day by day, moment by moment, each day some new disaster to see, hear, think about.

Now My children, these days you must think on Me. Stand still in Me. Hear my voice, obey My words as the world runs ahead. You are my Kingdom family and I love and protect you at all times. Your place is in Christ, in the shelter of the Rock.

Each day has troubles of its own, but in Christ is shelter, peace and provision: peace in the midst of the storm, shelter for your soul, food for your mind and water for your thirst,

Turn to me in the midst of this rushing world and know my joy, my way. It is my gift for you to enjoy.

DAY 9

SALVATION

'I tell you, now is the time of God's favour, now is the day of salvation.' *2 Corinthians 6:2b*
'She will give birth to a son, and you are to give him the name Jesus, because he will save his people from their sins.' *Matthew 1:21.*

I START THIS NEW MORNING in the usual way in praise and worship. It is always a lovely time. My mind is on another trip to the Beach as I turn to my morning reading which is taken from Psalm 118,
'Give thanks to the Lord, for He is good,
His love endures forever.'
The Lord is with me; I will not be afraid.
It is better to take refuge in the Lord than to trust in man.'

Once more, after worship and reading, I am suddenly on the Beach again. Now there is a thick mist over it. There are other shadowy figures on the Beach and I can see that they too are searching for something. What are they all looking for? The Lord answered the query in my mind.

'**They are looking for salvation, but in a mist --yet they must persevere.**'

'Lord, open the vision please. Help me to understand the meaning of this?'

'**Think My child!**'

Then I find I am walking on the sandy part of the Beach. The scene changes and as I look the mist clears. The people have gone and the Beach is deserted, but the memory of the mist and the shadowy figures is still with me. As I continue walking, I realise that the Lord has given me a hint of what the morning holds. I need help but continue to walk. I understand that it is to be a morning about salvation. This is what the shadowy figures had been seeking but they were in a mist, not seeing clearly. They were not walking in the light of truth. They did not know where or how to find salvation. The important thing was that they were seeking and if they truly persevered, they would not only find the truth but the way and the life, Jesus Christ Himself. Now I can ask the Lord about the jewel. How shall I recognise it? Where shall I look? His reply astonished me.

'**This morning, you are looking not for a stone, but a beautiful necklace - gold, with lovely jewels set into it. Look My child. Where will you find it?**'

And again I know the answer - I know where to look. It will be by the large rock.

'**When you find this necklace you can wear it. The jewels will display their magnificence. The gold will sparkle and be tranquil on your neck. The light and beauty of your necklace will be so attractive to others. They too will desire a necklace to wear. They know it will be beauty and direction for them on misty days and glory on sunny days. It will sit easily on them,**

easy to wear, full of delight, bringing total satisfaction and pleasure.'

So I make my way to the very large rock that I see in the distance. I had been there before looking for the kingdom pearl, and my understanding was that this massive outcrop of rock symbolized Jesus Christ.

The necklace is indeed by the rock, lying there, waiting for me, and I carefully put it on. It causes me to have an outburst of praise and worship;
'Lord this necklace is all sufficient and lovely. It is a delight to wear. It gives me confidence and pure pleasure and I know I am safe wearing it. It is my joy, my peace, my pleasure, my delight, my safety, my light, my protection in the storm, a sign upon me of Your good pleasure and delight in me.'

It is made of gold, with jewels set along its length; a thing of great beauty. I recognise some of the stones. They are like the ones I have already gathered on the Beach but there are more on it that I don't recognise. I see the black stone of grace - it sits so well surrounded by gold. Then there is the diamond of truth, and the blood red stone reminding me of the blood of Christ. I see the pearl of the kingdom reminding me of the King, the different coloured sapphires of glory, the lovely pure white peace stone, and the victory stone now mostly covered in its redness. The sapphire of faith is not there and I wondered why. (Some considerable time later I believe the Lord reminded me that it was not a jewel to wear but a jeweled pavement to walk on.)

Each jewel was set in gold which is associated with obedience and holiness, a fit setting, and there were new ones that I had not seen before. This makes me think and hope that there are many more mornings to come on the Beach. Now I need help from His Word to understand the significance of this.

Salvation

SALVATION - WHAT IS IT? Is it important? Should we want it and if so how do we get it? Is it for anyone, or conversely is it for everyone? The dictionary defines 'salvation' as:

- An act of saving or protecting from harm, risk, loss, destruction etc.
- The state of being saved or protected from harm, risk etc.
- A source, cause, or means of being saved or protected from harm, risk etc.
- Deliverance from the power and penalty of sin
- Redemption.

Surely we would all want this - wouldn't't we? These days the word 'Salvation' does not seem to be much in vogue. 'Have you been saved?' is rarely heard. Most people, especially in the West, appear to take it for granted that they will go to heaven one day, but not just yet they hope! Heaven is not thought of as having anything to do with Jesus Christ. It is rather their expectation of a friendly grandfatherly God, who will welcome them into a kind of paradise of their own description. In their estimation they have been good enough and deserve it.

Yet the Bible is full of salvation from beginning to end - sometimes just using the word and other times describing it.

The Bible tells us why we need it, how we receive it, who receives it, what it is, what it involves, what is expected by it, what are the benefits of it and what if you don't have it or don't want it? All of these questions are answered by God Himself in His Book - the Bible. Here is a helpful acronym for the word 'Bible':

BASIC **I**NSTRUCTIONS **B**EFORE **L**EAVING **E**ARTH

Just as any building needs a good foundation, so we find that the Old Testament lays the foundation for the New Testament.

The book of Genesis opens with the creation of a Garden, where all was perfection between man and God. The book of Revelation closes with the city of gold, coming down to the new earth, where man and creation are restored to perfection with God.

What happens in the books between explains the reason for, the need for, and the way into salvation. Restoration was needed because this perfect relationship between man and God was shattered when God's first created man, Adam, chose to follow his wife Eve into disobeying God and obeying Satan. This brought God's curse on man, the land and Satan. The Lord God said to Satan,
'Because you have done this,
Cursed are you above all the livestock, and all the wild animals!
You will crawl on your belly,
And you will eat dust all the days of your life.
And I will put enmity between you and the woman,
And between your offspring and hers;
He will crush your head,

And you will strike his heel.'[188]

The pain of childbearing for woman would be greatly multiplied, yet God pronounced that her desire would be for her husband and he would rule over her.[189] For the man, hard work would be needed to make a living; thorns and thistles would now grow and need to be dealt with, 'By the sweat of your brow you will eat your food until you return to the ground, since from it you were taken; for dust you are, and to dust you shall return.'[190]
The results of their disobedience were catastrophic:

- The penalty for sin resulted in death and they no longer had eternal life.
- They were turned out of their paradise-like surroundings, where all was provided for them and where they previously met with God each evening.
- Crucially they would now be unable to eat from the tree of life.

'And the Lord God said, 'The man has now become like one of us, knowing good and evil. He must not be allowed to reach out his hand and take also from the tree of life and eat, and live forever.'[191]

Even through this, God was showing mercy to fallen mankind. How appalling it would have been for man to have to

---

[188] Genesis 3:14-15
[189] Genesis 3:16
[190] Genesis 3:19
[191] Genesis 3:22

live on earth forever, as a sinner amongst sinners in an evil world.

So God banished them from the garden and they had to work in order to eat. A new life lay ahead which would be passed down to all mankind after them and would end in physical death. Eating from the forbidden tree was an act of deliberate rebellion. It was sin, which now became embedded in Adam's nature. We too understand this, as it is often the forbidden thing that draws us. However for Adam and the generations to follow this act was disastrous.

God had warned him that in the day that he ate he would die, and that is just what happened. He immediately became spiritually dead, separated from God. He had been created in the image of God, a tripartite being, spirit, soul and body. On that day the spirit part of man died. When Paul the Apostle wrote to the Ephesian Church, he said that at one time they had all been dead in their sins but now because of salvation, they had become alive.[192] Obviously it was not their body, nor soul, that was dead but the third part of their being, their spirit.

The forbidden tree in the garden was not 'the tree of good and evil', but 'the tree of the knowledge of good and evil.' The phrase 'knowing good and evil' implies not just a mental knowing but a more intimate experiential type of knowledge. The same Hebrew word 'yada' is used both for 'knowing' good and evil and for Adam's intimate 'knowing' of his wife resulting in the birth of Cain. So by eating of this fruit they entered into

---

[192] Ephesians 2:1

knowing and experiencing evil. When we read of some of the synonyms for evil, we recognise that evil has been active throughout all generations and all peoples, and we see evil fully evident in the world today.

A dictionary definition of evil uses these words: **'Base, beastly, corrupt, damnable, depraved, destructive, execrable, foul, hateful, heinous, iniquitous, malevolent, malicious, obscene, rancorous, repulsive, spiteful, vicious, vile, wicked and wrong.'**

Adam would have had no personal knowledge or any understanding of this before his disobedience or 'fall'. However, God had always known what the results from tasting the forbidden fruit would be. Death would not only mean the immediate death of the spirit of man, but the body would also physically die. This would become the inheritance of all mankind.

Many years later the level of world corruption and evil was so great that God brought about the great flood; 'The Lord saw how great man's wickedness on the earth had become, and that every inclination of the thoughts of his heart was only evil all the time. The Lord was grieved that he had made man on the earth, and his heart was filled with pain.'[193] Noah alone was saved because he found favour with God and his family was included in this physical saving or salvation.

Generations later God again chose a man called Abram, whom He would rename, Abraham. This man was a descendant of Shem, one of Noah's three sons. Now we begin to see God

---

[193] Genesis 6:5-6

setting in motion His plan for world redemption.

'The Lord said to Abram, 'Leave your country and your father's household and go to the land I will show you. I will make you into a great nation, and I will bless you; I will make your name great; and you will be a blessing. I will bless those who bless you, and whoever curses you I will curse; And all peoples on earth will be blessed through you.'[194]

This Covenant with Abraham is still being fulfilled today. The people or nations who bless Abraham's family - Israel, are themselves blessed. It is interesting to note that a high percentage of Nobel Prizewinners is Jewish, giving blessings to thousands.

The converse is also true, as those people or nations that curse 'the apple of God's eye' come under His judgement.

Abraham, who by Jewish tradition came from a wealthy family of idol makers in Ur of Chaldea, had an unforgettable meeting with the Living God. This caused him to leave his idol worship and his lucrative business and take a journey, led by God, to the land of Canaan. Throughout this time He was totally under the direction of God, whom he was just beginning to know and trust. Leaving Ur meant going from a most civilised city of two story homes, shops and businesses, education and many modern facilities to become a nomad - a tent dweller.

The writer to the Hebrews in the New Testament reflects that he had an inner vision. 'He was looking forward to the city with foundations, whose architect and builder is

---

[194] Genesis 12:1-3

God.'[195] Did he 'see' the New Jerusalem as described in the book of Revelation? In time he would become the Patriarch of the Jewish people, the nation that would be used in the genealogy of Jesus Christ, the Saviour of mankind.

The books of the Old Testament relate the history of God's dealings with this chosen man Abraham, His chosen descendants the Jewish nation, and His chosen land Israel. Then in the New Testament we arrive at the pinnacle of all history: the birth, death and resurrection of Jesus Christ, Yeshua, Salvation.

SALVATION COMES

When Joseph, the fiancé of Mary, knew about the pregnancy, he was both puzzled and troubled to the point of resolving to send her away and cancel the marriage agreement. As he slept on this, the Lord gave him a dream in which he saw an angel who said: "Joseph son of David, do not be afraid to take Mary home as your wife, because what has been conceived in her is from the Holy Spirit. She will give birth to a son, and you are to give him the name Jesus, because he will save his people from their sins."[196] Scripture continues, 'When Joseph woke up, he did what the angel of the Lord had commanded him, and took Mary home as his wife. But he had no union with her until she gave birth to a son. And he called His name Jesus.'[197]

---

[195] Hebrews 11:10
[196] Matthew 1:20b-21
[197] Matthew 1:24-25

How salvation would be accomplished is found in the book of Isaiah, which was written about seven hundred years before Christ's birth. Chapter 53, possibly one of the most well-known parts of the book, prophetically and most movingly describes Jesus as the suffering Servant and Man of sorrows. So accurate is Isaiah's revelation of Christ that one would think he had been at His trial and His execution. As a prophet and seer did Isaiah 'see' all this? One thing is certain; he was hearing the words of the Holy Spirit over seven hundred years before the birth of Jesus Christ, foretelling that He would be a guilt offering for many and bear their iniquities.

How do we know that this was written before the time of Jesus? In 1947, a shepherd boy who was tending his flock in the Qumran desert discovered many clay containers in which were found ancient scrolls. These became known as the 'Dead Sea Scrolls' and proved to be a great archaeological find, giving veracity to much of the Old Testament of the Bible. This included an almost intact scroll of the book of Isaiah, dated at 150-100 BC. Isaiah himself dated the period of his own ministry by naming the four kings of Judah under whom he served – Uzziah, Jotham, Ahaz and Hezekiah, who reigned from 792 to 686 BC.

This scroll is on view in the Museum of the Shrine of the Book in Jerusalem and may be accessed on –line.

Chapter 53 of the book of Isaiah graphically describes the events of the Cross. Here is just a portion of it;
'Surely He took up our infirmities
and carried our sorrows;
yet we considered him stricken by God
smitten by him, and afflicted.
But He was pierced for our transgressions,
he was crushed for our iniquities;
the punishment that brought us peace was upon him,
and by his wounds we are healed.
We all, like sheep, have gone astray,
each of us has turned to his own way;
and the Lord has laid on him the iniquity of us all.'[198]

There is more: He is likened to a lamb that is led to be slaughtered, a lamb that is silent, as Jesus was before his accusers at His trial. Even the fact that Christ would have a rich man's grave was pictured further on in verse 9. All of this was prophesied by Isaiah about seven hundred years before Jesus Christ was born.

It is also interesting that the year of the discovery of the 'Dead Sea Scrolls' which speaks descriptively of the Messiah, is also the year initiating the birth of the State of Israel.

Shortly after Christ's resurrection and ascension to the Father, the Apostle Peter began to teach about Salvation. It was the day of Pentecost and the Holy Spirit had come upon all the disciples. Crowds had gathered outside the house having heard

---

[198] Isaiah 53:4-6

the sound of the rushing wind. They were puzzled when the disciples came out, speaking in many different languages, and even more amazed when they realised that these Jews were speaking in the languages of the crowd, who came from 'every nation under heaven.' Peter preached to them, explaining much of the events of the past weeks and the importance of Christ's death and resurrection. He brought the two words 'Salvation' and 'Jesus' together saying, 'Salvation is found in no one else, for there is no other name under heaven given to men by which we must be saved.'[199] Had his hearers made the connection? Did they remember that the Hebrew word for 'Salvation,' used so very often in the Old Testament and with which they were familiar is 'YESHUA,' Jesus?

Another lovely Hebrew word used throughout the Old Testament is 'chesed' which means mercy, kindness, faithfulness and loving kindness, and this perfectly describes God's salvation.

RIGHTEOUS WRATH AND RIGHTEOUS MERCY

Wrath is rarely heard or spoken about these days. No longer do we see men walking in our shopping centers with boards on their shoulders saying, 'The wages of sin is death' and 'Prepare to meet thy God' How would they be viewed by 21st Century shoppers?

---

[199] Acts 4:12

Interestingly the Baptist Church in Widcombe, Bath has the following painted in large white letters on the tiles of the roof:

Prepare to meet your God.
You must be born again.
We have redemption through His blood.
Christ died for our sins.[200]

    A visiting evangelist about the year 1900 had suggested that the members of the Church display these words, and they have remained ever since. Apparently it has quite an effect on those flying overhead, and it can be seen when driving past.

    My thoughts turned to praising him for my salvation and I began to realise how all the jewels that He had shown me on the Beach were encapsulated in Salvation: His Grace, His Truth, His shed Blood, His Peace, His Victory and Faith.
'Lord you are amazing. You teach me truth, Your truth in such a wonderful way. I do thank You with all my heart. And there is still much more to learn. You open Your treasure chest to me and invite me to take from it. I will be covered with precious jewels from You!'
'My child don't we have fun together.'
'Absolutely Lord!'
'I give you My full blessing. Enjoy!'

---

[200] Amos 4:12, John 3:7, Ephesians 1:7, and 1 Peter 3:18.
Permission given by Widcombe Baptist Church, Bath UK

Prophetic Word

My dear child, My dear children,
You are increasingly aware in your spirit of a moving on into new times - times you have not known before – times you have longed for – times of knowing My presence in a deeper way, and a time of a shift into My plans and My purposes.
This time and these times are moving forward into your time, and you will begin to understand more fully the signs of the times. Warfare abounds world – wide and this is just a shadow of the warfare that rages in the heavens. Yet you My children are so very safe in Me. and I call you to remain and to abide in Me. Abide in Me in new ways. Come to Me and you too will hear My voice even as a whisper.

Do not fear and do not be discouraged. You know that My light in you dispels all darkness and I have provided such protection for you - Your daily armour covering you - the blood of the Lamb your total atonement. So be prepared my flock for new ways which are old ways, as everything is shaken. You will move out of stale habits and new, better ways will take their place. These ways will be fresh and invigorating in the Holy Spirit as you place Me, your Lord God Almighty, as first in your life, knowing Me as your First Love. Come and bathe in the Water of Life. Be refreshed in My Holy Spirit My children. Walk on, out of the shallows and into the depths where My Spirit will hold you up. Come My children, do not hesitate. Step out in the faith I give you - yet be circumspect and wise with the wisdom I give you. Redeem the time. Be bold and be expectant. My mercy and My peace are ever flowing. Allow My Holy Spirit to really fill you and you will know such fellowship with Me and with each other. You will remember your First love for Me and My love will fill you. Amen.

Praise

DAY 10

PRAISE

'In almost everything that touches our everyday life on earth; God is pleased when we're pleased. He wills that we be as free as birds to soar and sing our maker's praise without anxiety.'   *A.W. Tozer*
'If you are humble, nothing will touch you, neither praise nor disgrace, because you know what you are.'   *Mother Teresa*

AFTER A TIME OF PRAISE I asked,
'Lord, am I to look for the praise stone this morning?'
'Yes My child - you will love this - it's a lovely morning. Praise is wonderful.'
And it is a wonderful morning. I'm back on the Beach. The sky and the sea are blue, the sand and pebbles beneath my feet are warm. Although I know that pebbles are hard, these pebbles are almost soft, easy to walk on. Perfect. Walking and talking with the Lord.
 'Lord, to praise You is the most wonderful thing.'
'Praise accompanies salvation child, doesn't it.'
'Absolutely Lord. What can I do but praise You when I consider my salvation? And there is more to come, the final salvation at the end of days. Wonder of Wonders. Yes. Praise in all its different colours, different facets.'

'You have understood it My child. So look for the rainbow coloured stone. It is a glorious stone. Each colour glows and sparkles. It is a thing of beauty to you and to Me.'
'Lord what a wonderful way to think of praise. There are many different things to praise You for and so many different situations in which to praise You.'

This morning's walk is leisurely - no problems. I am confident that I shall soon find the rainbow stone, enjoying the Beach, feeling as if I'm on holiday. Yes. I find it easily amongst the pebbles. Its glowing colours make it stand out. As I pick it up, outrageous and extravagant praise and worship begins to flow.

'Picking up this praise jewel brings warmth and coolness, the feel and knowledge of Your Presence, Your hand in mine, and glorious music - a release to dance before You. A quietness as I am on my face before You. Surely Lord one day I will be there before You, praising You in a wonderful and glorious way.'

And there was more as the Holy Spirit continued to bring worship and praise to my spirit for quite some time. Then He said,

'You see from this morning child, that praise precedes the Word and praise in the Spirit opens the way. The Word without praise is - words, but preceded by praise, the Word is bathed in the Holy Spirit, in wisdom and in hearing My voice. So isn't this a wonder My child. And you are enjoying this aren't you.'
'Indeed Lord. I have always known that praise is wonderful. This is lovely. So peaceful. So satisfying. So full of nearness with you. Yet I know that even so, there is more, more of You. What now Lord?'
'Go to My Word. See how much praise there is in the Old Covenant. How much more will be in the New Covenant, when the Blood of Jesus has been shed for you, forgiving, washing

and cleansing you of all your sin; and the Holy Spirit poured out from on high to be your Helper.'

'Lord I see now that there is an abundance of praise in your Word, and there are so many different meanings and flavours of praise. Which to choose....?'

'I will lead you My child.

Praise

It seemed good to start by looking in the Old Testament. When the nation of Israel was walking in obedience with the Lord God - praise and worship flowed. Singers were appointed in large numbers to lead praise especially during important gathering, often singing, 'He is good; his love endures forever,'[201] and musicians praised God with psalteries, trumpets, cymbals, harps and lyres.

When Solomon brought the Ark of the Covenant into the newly built Temple, there was an outstanding time of prayer, sacrifice and worship. A large choir singing these words was accompanied by the instrumentalists, which included one hundred and twenty priests playing trumpets. The cloud of the Lord's glory so filled the Temple that the priests could not stand in His presence to perform their service; [202]the effect of worship!

LEAH'S STORY

This is the story of a very sad woman called Leah, and the outcome of her sacrificial praise.

Abraham's grandson Jacob had two unhappy wives, each one

---

[201] 2 Chronicles 5:13b
[202] 1Kings 8:10 -11

jealous of the other: Rachel, who was loved dearly by Jacob, had no children, which caused her to say to Jacob one day, 'Give me children or I will die!' His other wife Leah, had no problem in bearing children, but was unloved by her husband. In fact Jacob, thinking he was marrying the love of his life, Rachel, had been tricked into first marrying the older sister Leah, by her father. This was not a good start to their marriage.[203]

Leah thought that after having her third son, Jacob would love her but it was not so. When her fourth son was born, Leah decided that she needed to praise God despite her unhappiness. She praised God and called the baby Judah, which means Praise.

She would not have known that amongst this baby's descendants would be the most famous kings of Israel. We can trace King David's ancestry to Judah in Matthew's Gospel Chapter 1, followed closely by King Solomon his son and eventually the King of kings - Jesus Christ.[204] Matthew's genealogy shows we can see that a whole line of kings came from a baby named 'Praise', whose mother put her sadness to one side and concentrated on praising God.

Leah stopped having children for a while, but later conceived again so that eventually she had six sons and a daughter. All six sons eventually became heads of the tribes of Israel along with the other six sons of Jacob. The nation of Israel was about to be born.

So why is this story so remarkable? It shows that praise

---

[203] Genesis 29:16-27
[204] Matthew 1:1-17 and Hebrews 7:14a

is possible in all situations, even those emotionally difficult circumstances. The Bible calls it the sacrifice of praise, praising God when there seems to be nothing in our situation for which to praise Him. It is a sacrifice, it costs us something and God rewards genuine praise, quite often by answering desperate prayer.

What happened to Rachel? After some time she had a son called Joseph. We learn from Scripture, that his father Jacob loved him more than all his other sons because he was born to him in his old age. Sadly this favouritism became unbearable to the other sons, particularly when Jacob gave Joseph a very special coloured robe. Out of their jealousy his step brothers decided to kill Joseph. However, when the time came, Judah, Praise, was the one who persuaded them to spare his life and sell him into slavery to some passing traders.[205]

The story of Joseph who rose from being a slave in Egypt, to being Pharaoh's second in command is found in Genesis Chapter 37 and Chapters 39 to 48. Years later, Jacob and his household of seventy moved to Egypt at Joseph's and Pharaoh's invitation. They grew and multiplied greatly in numbers, staying there for four hundred years until Moses led them out towards the Promised Land. There they became the nation of Israel and were known as Jews, after the name 'Judah.' So both Leah and Rachel bore sons that had a major impact on Jewish history.

It is interesting that the Bible records several incidents of women who were childless. Not only were their situations

---

[205] Genesis 37:1-36

turned around by God's grace, but their first born sons became instrumental in God's eternal purposes. We have Abraham and Sarah with Isaac as an example, also this last account of Jacob, Rachel and Joseph. Several hundred years later we see how another wife, Hannah, found herself in a similar situation to Rachel.

In 1 Samuel Chapters 1 and 2, we read of another two wives, Peninnah having sons and daughters, and the other, Hannah, the loved wife, being childless. Not only that but she was always being taunted and provoked by Peninnah. Hannah shed many tears and her husband Elkanah said, 'Hannah, why do you weep. And why do you not eat and why is your heart sad? Am I not better to you than ten sons?'
So Hannah went to her source of help, the Lord, and made a vow. If He would give her a son, then she would give him back to the Lord. After this she conceived and gave birth to Samuel. She fulfilled her promise by dedicating him to God when he was a small child and leaving him at the Temple in the care of the high priest Eli. Here the boy Samuel heard God speak in the night and began to recognise the voice of the Lord. As Hannah was leaving this precious child with Eli she brought a hymn of praise to God, some of it being sung even today:

'There is no-one holy like the Lord;
there is no-one besides You;
there is no Rock like our God.'[206]

Samuel grew up to be a prophet and a judge in Israel, teaching and leading the nation in Godliness. And Hannah? She

---

[206] 1 Samuel 2:2

had three more sons and two daughters.

Luke's Gospel in the New Testament tells of two Godly old and childless people -Zachariah the priest and his wife Elizabeth. Zachariah was attending to his duties in the temple when the angel Gabriel appeared before him, which terrified him. The angel began to tell him that he and Elizabeth would indeed have a son who would be great in the sight of God and would turn many of the sons of Israel back to God.

Zachariah thought that he and Elizabeth were now well past the age for bearing children and was most unsure about it saying, 'How shall I know this?' So Gabriel gave him a sign: he would be unable to speak until the child was born. This sign was given because he had not believed the angel's words. When the child was born he was to be called John. This all came to pass. As soon as Zachariah could speak and name his son, he began to praise God. John, this special child, was John the Baptist, the one who would prepare the way for the Messiah.[207]

When we want to praise the Lord, we often turn to the book of Psalms, many of which were written by David who was called 'The sweet psalmist of Israel'[208] Time and again we find Psalms that express our own thoughts and prayers. David was an outrageous, consistent and faithful man of praise, in good times and in bad. Psalm 23, 'The Lord is my Shepherd' is one that has brought comfort, worship, hope and direction to many people worldwide.

---

[207] Luke 1:5-20
[208] 2 Samuel 23:1

EARTHQUAKE PRAISE

In the New Testament, we find a time when praise brought a most unexpected result. The Apostles Paul and Silas had been thrown into jail in Philippi after being stripped and severely flogged. Their feet were chained and how easily they could have said, 'Why Lord?' They had previously been shown in a vision to go to Macedonia, so they knew they were in the right place, Philippi being the leading city there.

This was not a good start to spreading the Gospel, nevertheless Paul and Silas chose to praise God. These two men knew how to offer the sacrifice of praise, which the Lord will always honour in some way.

Praising God in difficult times will lead us out of the temptations of self- pity and possible discouragement or despair. God may not bring a physical earthquake, but He can shake the situation we are in and bring release. Thus we read, 'About midnight Paul and Silas were praying and singing hymns to God, and the other prisoners were listening to them. Suddenly there was such a violent earthquake that the foundations of the prison were shaken. At once all the prison doors flew open and everybody's chains came loose. The jailer woke up and when he saw the prison doors open he drew his sword and was about to kill himself because he thought the prisoners had escaped. But Paul shouted, "Don't harm yourself! We are all here!"'[209]

This caused the now trembling jailer to say, "Sirs, what must I

---

[209] Acts 16:25-28

do to be saved?"[210]

God has His own way of leading circumstances, and out of this situation the Church at Philippi was born. The jailer and his family then became Christians and would have been amongst the congregation of the new young Church.

One particular sacrifice of praise became a reality to a certain family. They were at a Christian Conference and at the end of his talk; the speaker gave the call to salvation to the congregation. Streams of young people went forward. When the family realised that their daughter was not amongst them, they chose to praise God, singing as the band played, 'We bring the Sacrifice of Praise.' Several hours later, this daughter went to them and announced that she had been born again, and was to be baptised the following day.

We can never 'outgive' God. Our sacrifices to Him are nothing compared with the gifts He showers back on us. Years later, this young woman is a blessing to many.

HEAVENLY PRAISE

Toward the end of the book of Revelation, the Apostle John describes the scene in heaven of outrageous praise and worship. The fervor of it is reminiscent of Psalm 150 but more so. A vast crowd shouts, 'Hallelujah! Salvation and glory and power belong to our God for true and just are his judgements.'[211]

From the throne a voice rings out, 'Praise our God all

---

[210] Acts 16:30b
[211] Revelation 19:1b

his servants, all who fear him both great and small.'[212] Then John heard something like the voice of a vast multitude, like the sound of cascading waters, and like the rumbling of loud thunder which was saying this,
'Hallelujah! –
For our Lord God Almighty reigns.
Let us rejoice and be glad and give him glory!
For the wedding of the Lamb has come, and his bride has made herself ready.'[213]

Maybe in heaven we will be surprised at the passion and volume of praise and worship that is given to God.

TRIALS AND TESTS

'Fire tests the purity of silver and gold, but a person is tested by being praised.' Proverbs 27:21 NLT

When gold or silver is being purified, great heat is used to bring up the dross from the molten metals, so that it can be scooped out. In the same way that this process brings purity to the metals, so the 'fires' of trial and difficulty can be instrumental in bringing us into a new maturity. We are made holy by God as the dross of hidden, unknown or accepted sin is dealt with. The key is submitting to God in these times and allowing Him to do His perfect work in us and not fighting the situation in our own strength. Out of such situations usually comes praise to God as

---

[212] Revelation 19:5
[213] Revelation 19:6b-8a

we realise that what He has allowed, has taught us many lessons.

Human praise is a test too. When it is given to someone, it brings a test to the person's integrity. What is the effect of the praise, does it bring encouragement or pride? Whether it is open and deserved approbation or flattery, how we handle it is important. As Christians we need to be able to give and receive encouragement in the right way. Flattery is not helpful.

DENY OR DIE

Many people including the rulers in Jesus' time heard the Gospel, saw the miracles and believed, but they did not openly confess their beliefs. They feared being put out of the synagogue, which was both the religious and the social center of the community. They would not want to be excommunicated. Jesus said that everyone who confessed Him before men, He would confess before the Father in heaven, but anyone who denied Him before men, He would deny before his Father in heaven. [214]

Would we want Him to disown us before the Father or would we prefer that He acknowledge us? May we all know the power of the Holy Spirit and the grace of God in these situations so that we remain faithful.

The temptation to deny Christ is a present reality today in many countries. People are warned that they will face death or serious persecution if they follow Christ. Nevertheless, there are thousands who are turning to Him, having seen Jesus in

---

[214] Matthew 10:32-33

their dreams and visions. They are overwhelmed by His amazing love for them and become believers and disciples themselves. Those who face losing life or family know that the One who purchased Redemption for them also faced the same decisions.

Thankfully the grace of God is strong and we can rely on Him to give wisdom and strength. Help may always be found in the Word of God, from the fellowship of the saints and from His wonderful love. It is a good thing to remember all those who are suffering under persecution at this time and pray for them.

As we draw nearer to the second coming of the Lord Jesus, we cannot help but notice an increase in the lawlessness, sinfulness and godlessness that Paul spoke of in Chapter 3 of his second letter to Timothy. We look to the Lord, knowing that the God we worship is King over all the earth and He, our Rock, has all in His hands and we will praise Him.

'Time to go My child. You see that praise could go on forever.'

And so it does! 'Amen Lord.'

PRAISE MY SOUL THE KING OF HEAVEN
To his feet thy tribute bring;
Ransomed, healed, restored forgiven
Who like me his praise should sing.
Praise Him! Praise Him! (x2)
Praise the everlasting King!

Praise Him for his grace and favour
To our fathers in distress;
Praise him still the same for ever,
Slow to chide and swift to bless.
Praise Him! Praise Him!(x2)
Glorious in His faithfulness.

Father-like He tends and spares us
Well our feeble frame He knows;
In his hands He gently bears us,
Rescues us from all our foes.
Praise Him! Praise Him! x2
Widely as His mercy flows.

Angels help us to adore Him;
Ye behold him face to face;
Sun and moon bow down before Him;
Dwellers all in time and space:
Praise Him! Praise Him,
Praise Him! Praise Him!
Praise with us the God of grace.

Henry Lyte 1793-1847

DAY 11

LOVE

'Love is not love which alters when it alteration finds.'
Shakespeare
'A friend is someone who knows all about you and still loves you.'
Elbert Hubbard
'Love is patient, love is kind. It does not envy.'
1 Corinthians 13: 4a

My hour of worship started with this lovely hymn, written by William Featherston, it is believed when he was 12 or 16 years old.

'My Jesus I love Thee, I know Thou art mine.
For Thee all the follies of sin I resign.
My gracious Redeemer, My Saviour art Thou,
If ever I loved Thee My, Jesus, 'tis now.'
William Featherston 1864

Afterwards I asked Him,
'Why does this time with You go so quickly Lord?'
There is no time in My presence child, only now. Which stone would you like today child?'

'Lord, I love You. You choose.'
Then the stone of love. You have chosen!
'Wonderful, Lord! How do I recognise it? By the colour?'
'You will know it by its shape - not its colour.'
  So once again I am walking along the Beach, looking amongst the pebbles for a special jewel and trusting the Lord to lead me to it. Then I see it. This must be the love jewel. The Lord observed that I had seen it and said,
'This is a beautiful jewel. I have shown it to you.'
  Of course, it is heart shaped, the colour is the deepest darkest red and it is already set in gold. It is such a beautiful jewel to look at and knowing the love that it represents makes it even more desirable.
'Wear this stone My child. Know My deepest love at all times. Allow My love to flow out from you. Others will see this love and be drawn to Me. They will desire to wear this stone also, to know My love for themselves. See its beauty My dear child, the depth of it ….'
  As I turn it over in my hand I can see just how rich and lovely it is, and the gold setting enriches its beauty.
The Lord began to speak again.
  'We could talk of My love forever. My love is richer, deeper, more wonderful than any love that you have ever known. You can rest in and relax in my love. You can be at peace in My love - dance in My love - smile in My love, be warmed by My love - be separated unto Me – yes, be holy. All that is pure and undefiled is in My love. You can see yourself in My love for that is your place in Me. My love is all encompassing - it stretches in all directions - goes

before you - walks at your side - protects you from behind. Wherever you walk, - My love is with you.'

The psalmist David knew the truth of this. He said 'Lord, where can I go from Your presence?'[215]

'Yes child. I Am always with you. I Am your love. This jewel you will wear on your forehead. My love is on your head, covering your mind. It is your protection, so wherever you go My love is on you from head to foot.'

'Lord I bow before you. Words are not enough.'

'My love is your chief weapon for your task as Watchman. It is part of the Sword of the Spirit. It is the hilt - the handle - and it brings victory. You hold my Word with love. If you tried to wield the Sword without the hilt you would hurt yourself, so you need to hold the handle of love, My love, at all times, then My Word can achieve what I desire, the battle is won- and you are safe and secure.'

'This is wonderful Lord. Holy Spirit please remind me of this when I am led into battle. May your love enfold me and Your love lead me.'

'Here is a truth for you My child. Yes. You know why this stone is the deepest, most beautiful red.' (I knew the Lord was speaking about His sacrifice of love.) 'My child you will see how My love overcomes, wins battles, brings healing, comforts in sorrows, brings hope, dispels despair, brings joy -peace -all this much more. My love never fails and is always victorious.'

It was time to seek the Word again.

---

[215] Psalm 139:7

Love

Love

LOVE. We all know what love is - don't we? Here is the Bible's description of love and surely this is how we want to be loved. When we read this we also recognise that these words describe how Jesus wants us to love others.

Love is patient.
Love is kind.
Love does not envy.
Love does not boast.
Love is not proud.
Love is not self-seeking.
Love is not easily angered.
Love keeps no record of wrongs.
Love does not delight in evil but rejoices with the truth.
Love always protects,
Always trusts,
Always hopes,
Always perseveres.
Love never fails. And now these three remain: faith, hope and love. But the greatest of these is love.[216]
Can we love like this?

---

[216] 1 Corinthians 13:4-8a

HIS LOVE-OUR LOVE

There is only one way to begin to love others like this and fulfill Christ's commandment.[217] We need His perfect love in us, a love that will bubble up and overflow to others. We all know that some people are easy to love- even so we can't completely fulfil the 1 Corinthians 13 list. Others are disagreeable, aggravating, selfish, disappointing, hard work, liars and even evil in outlook. But of these two descriptions, which one fits us?

The Book says that Christ died for us, the ungodly, and God showed his love for us by sending Christ to die for us while we were sinners.[218] We begin to understand that God's love is a supernatural love and if we are to love like this, we also need the gift of supernatural love. We cannot do it in our own strength. It's just not in us! Yet according to His Word, this kind of love is in us. How is this possible? The answer comes through being born again.

When we are born again, it means just that. We are born all over again, a new start in life. We become a new person, transformed, and we begin to know the truth that the love of God is released in our hearts through the Holy Spirit.[219] Paul teaches that 'if anyone is in Christ he is a new creation; the old has gone the new has come!'[220]

So we find to our amazement that we have new outlooks on life, new desires to please Him and not ourselves,

---

[217] John 15:12
[218] Romans 5:6-7
[219] Romans 5:5
[220] 2 Corinthians 5:17

new interests like reading the Bible and praying, new friends and a new love for others - a God kind of love! We also discover that the Holy Spirit becomes our power-house in all this. He is the source of our ability to love.

After His resurrection, Jesus told His disciples to wait in Jerusalem for the special promise of God that He had told them about. This was another baptism, not that of water and done by man, but that of the Holy Spirit and coming from Him. 'For John baptised with water, but in a few days you will be baptised with the Holy Spirit.'[221]

Jesus continued by saying that they would receive power when the Holy Spirit came upon them. This promise which was fulfilled on the day of Pentecost is also promised to believers today. Here is how we are able to love others with God's love.

He puts His nature in us and we can have the power of the Holy Spirit to help us. Love is part of the fruit of the Holy Spirit[222] and just as fruit just grows whilst on the branch, so this gift of love grows in the one who is joined to the Lord Jesus. The gift of His love in us is able to flow out to others and over the years we learn how to share His ways.

Jesus simplifies it by saying that we should treat others in the same way we like to be treated. He goes on to say that even the ungodly can love those who love them, but believers are called to love their enemies and do good to them, even lending to them without expecting anything back.

---

[221] Acts 1:4-5
[222] Galatians 5:22-23

'Then your reward will be great, and you will be sons of the Most High, because He is kind to the ungrateful and wicked. Be merciful just as your Father is merciful.'[223]

There are several words for love in the Greek language, each describing a different type of love. In the English language we can love our mother, our children, our spouse, our dog, ice-cream, going on holiday and a hundred other things, all with the same word. Not so in Greek. The Greek word for the 'all encompassing' love of God is 'agape.' and is distinguished from brotherly or friendship love (philea) or sensual love (eros). However, 'agape' is the highest of all the types of love and is the love that Jesus has for us. It is selfless and sacrificial, a love that shows itself in action.

This is the love that God showed when He sent His Son to die for us. It is interesting that when Jesus talked with Peter after His resurrection He used two different types of love, which in the Greek text become obvious. (Many Bibles have end notes that explain the different Greek words used here.)

The following conversation takes place when Jesus appears to a group of His disciples after His resurrection. They were on the lake of Galilee, disappointed because after a night's fishing they had caught nothing. As they approached the shore a man called out telling them to cast their nets on the right side of the boat. This they did, not knowing that it was Jesus, and caught such a large number of fish that they could scarcely haul it into the boat.

Then John realised who it was and said to Peter, "It is the

---

[223] Luke 6:31-36

Lord."[224] Immediately, Peter put on his outer garment and plunged into the sea, desperate for Jesus. There was a charcoal fire ready, with bread and fish. As the rest of the disciples neared the shore, Jesus invited them all to bring more fish and eat with Him. Peter then helped bring in the net, and after eating breakfast the following conversation ensued.

Jesus asked him, 'Do you love Me Peter?' using the word 'agape' but Peter replied with 'philea', 'You know I love You Lord.' Then a second time Jesus asked, again using the same word 'agape', and Peter replied again saying, 'You know I 'phileo' You.' Yet once more Jesus asked; 'Do you love Me Peter?' but this time He used the word 'phileo'. Do you love Me in a brotherly, friendly sort of way? To which Peter could comfortably reply, 'Yes. You know I love you.' Each time Peter replied, the Lord commissioned him to feed and shepherd His sheep and lambs.[225]

This was a time of total restoration for Peter. Before the crucifixion he had protested his love for Jesus to the point of being willing to die for Him. But as Jesus had predicted, only hours after this protestation of love, he had equally powerfully cursed and sworn three times that he did not even know Jesus. Then the rooster crowed and Jesus turned and looked at him. Peter was devastated. Undone.

Now, on this beach and by the charcoal fire, Jesus led him through a time of forgiveness and restoration. Had Peter been thinking about the last charcoal fire at which he had warmed himself, the place where he had cursed and denied his

---

[224] John 21:7
[225] John 21:1-22

Lord? Jesus however continued, indicating to Peter that indeed he *would* give his life and it would be in a similar way to Christ, by crucifixion. 'But follow Me,' Jesus said.

By now Peter was realising that by these three questions his three denials had been forgiven; he was truly accepted and loved by Jesus. This love was the 'agape' God kind of love - His kind of love for us.

WORDS ONLY?

Treating others the way we would like to be treated covers the list in 1Corinthians13. We realise that some sort of action is needed to really love, even if it is the negative action of not saying or not doing something to retaliate. To say we love someone without showing it in some way is empty. Words only can be cheap and meaningless. Jesus Himself said that if we love Him we will keep His commandments. In practice, His wonderful love for us causes us to really want to follow Him and we slowly learn that He can give us what we need.

There is the story of Corrie Ten Boom, who after being released from the concentration camp in Germany, came face to face with the woman who had been responsible for her beloved sister's death. This woman, once a brutal camp guard, was now a Christian. Corrie knew she had to not only forgive her but to love her and accept her as a sister in Christ. She had such a battle but once again, the grace of God prevailed.[226]

---

[226] Ten Boom, C. Sherill J &,E, 1971

THE PERFECT CHURCH?

One of the places that Paul visited was Ephesus. He spent two years there teaching, preaching and building up the new Church. When he first arrived he found a few believers but they had not been water baptised into Christ nor baptised in the Holy Spirit. He was able to lead them in these baptisms and they became the core of the new Church.[227] During these two years this congregation grew in numbers and maturity. Having Paul as the resident Apostle and teacher must have been illuminating.

He wrote to the church some years later. This Ephesian letter, found in the New Testament, describes the blessings that come to believers. It is full of doctrinal truth, instructions for family counsel and then finally the spiritual armour available to the Christian. All of this is unsurpassed and bathed in his love for the fellowship there in Ephesus. His prayers in the first chapter are full of encouragement for us also.

This Church had everything and if it were here today, would no doubt be held up as a model for all Churches to follow. Having had the blessing of Paul with them for two years, they were further blessed when after Paul's death the Apostle John settled in Ephesus and according to tradition, was accompanied by Mary, Jesus' mother.

Years later when this Ephesian Church was well established John, now in his nineties (and the last of the early disciples,) was imprisoned on the island of Patmos for his faith. Here he had a series of visions from Jesus Christ which are

---

[227] Acts 19:1-6

found in the book of Revelation. Included in the vision were letters from Jesus to seven local Churches in Asia Minor.

The first of these letters was to the Church at Ephesus and in it the Lord commended them on so many things. They were hard working and persevered, they had not tolerated false apostles who had made their way to the Church and tried to set themselves up. They had dealt with evil men and not allowed them to remain. They had not grown weary in difficult circumstances and had remained faithful to the Gospel message. It sounds as though in modern day terms they had a good disciplined evangelistic, lively Church with prayer meetings, Bible studies, and sound doctrine - reliable in many respects.

They also hated the ways of the Nicolaitans which Christ also hated. There is much conflicting thought and tradition regarding the Nicolaitans, and suffice to say that Christ hated their ways and applauded the Ephesian Church for their similar stance.

What possible fault could the Lord find in this all but perfect Church? Here is His sorrow,
'I hold this against you: You have forsaken your first love. Remember the height from which you have fallen! Repent and do the things you did at first. If you do not repent, I will come to you and remove your lampstand stand from its place.'[228]
The Lord was looking for their first love and not finding it. They were in danger of losing their lampstand – the Church, in Ephesus.

---

[228] Revelation 2:4-5

DREAMS AND VISIONS

News is emerging of thousands of people from many countries who are seeing Jesus in dreams and visions. The supreme Love that emanates from Jesus to them is so overwhelming that they are captivated by Him and want to follow Him. Here is part of a testimony from one such lady.

'Jesus walked with me alongside a lake, and He told me how much He loves me. I think my husband loved me at one time. But the love I felt in my dream - His love - was different than anything I've ever experienced. I've never felt such peace in my heart. I didn't want to leave and He said 'I love you Noor, I have given everything for you. I died for you.' [229]

She was led to speak with a Christian about her experience and he answered her many questions and explained the Gospel to her. He also brought two questions to her; was she willing to be persecuted for Jesus and was she willing to die for Him? She began to understand the cost, but she had seen Jesus and talked with Him. She could not deny the One she had seen and talked with and she knew quite well that she was putting her life and probably her family's life on the line. She later received salvation.

There are many people having similar experiences. They meet with the Lord Jesus in a vision and are captivated by His love for them. He died for them.

---

[229] Doyle, 2006, p146

THE SPLENDOUR OF LOVE

'First love' - how do we describe it? When we have experienced it we know what it is. Between a young man and woman it is obvious to others. The way they always want to be together, how they talk of each other to their friends and look at each other. Nothing is too hard to please the other, letters and texts are precious and re-read many times.

And first love with Jesus Christ, how does this show itself? Surely in similar ways. We want to spend a lot of time in His presence, often thinking about Him, in prayer and worship at odd moments day or night. We love to read His Word and learn to hear Him speak to us through it. Being with those who share our faith is a delight and we often tell others of our experiences with God. He is the centre of our life - the Lord of our life.

This is the sort of love that Jesus looks for above all in His people, the Church. His love for us is faithful, true, eternal and absolute. He is merciful and compassionate. He understands our weaknesses and is always ready to forgive and restore us. The Lord God is our most faithful Father, who loves His children without limit and nothing can separate us from this love. Paul, by the power of the Holy Spirit, is persuaded that 'neither death nor life, nor angels, nor principalities, nor powers, nor things present nor things to come, nor height nor depth, nor any other created thing, shall be able to separate us from the love of God, which is in Jesus Christ.'[230]

---

[230] Romans 8:38-39

What a wonderful thing is the love of God poured into us. We are so undeserving, yet He loves us. With much to think about, my morning comes to an end and I thank the Lord Jesus for His wonderful love.
His reply, and to all His children is;
'I love you My child.'

Love

MY JESUS, I LOVE THEE, I know Thou art mine.
For Thee all the follies of sin I resign;
My gracious Redeemer, my Saviour art Thou;
If ever I loved Thee, My Jesus, 'tis now.

I love thee because Thou hast first loved me,
And purchased my pardon on Calvary's tree;
I love thee for wearing the thorns on Thy brow;
If ever I loved Thee, my Jesus 'tis now.

I'll love thee in life, I will love thee in death,
And praise thee as long as Thou lendest me breath;
And say when the death dew lies cold on my brow,
If ever I loved Thee, my Jesus 'tis now.

In mansions of glory and endless delight,
I'll ever adore Thee in heaven so bright;
I'll sing with the glittering crown on my brow,
If ever I loved Thee, my Jesus 'tis now.
William R. Featherston 1848-1875

DAY 12

OBEDIENCE

'No man commands safely unless he has learned well how to obey.'
Thomas a Kempis
'We take captive every thought to make it obedient to Christ.'
2 Corinthians 10:5b
'As an earring of gold, or an ornament of fine gold, is a wise man's rebuke to a listening ear.' *Proverbs 25:12*

As I look through the window very early on this cold February morning, I see the stars shining – crisp - beautiful, in a clear dark sky and I am automatically drawn to one of the psalms.
'The heavens declare the glory of God;
And the firmament shows His handiwork
.Day unto day utters speech,
And night unto night reveals knowledge.
There is no speech nor language where their voice is not heard.
Their line is gone out through all the earth,

And their words to the end of the world.[231]

I remember learning these words in school when I was seven. Then the words rolled off our young tongues like music, but now they speak wisdom and beauty. Such is the Word of God. This leads me straight into praise.

Afterwards I heard the Lord say: **This is a time to be still and know that I am God.'**

'Yes Lord. Thank you Jesus for all You did at the Cross. I just need to tuck up with You Lord - no striving - just sitting with You dear Lord - enjoying this praise and music with You.
In Your presence Lord I have everything, all that I need or want. This is lovely Lord, and one day I will be with You, listening and enjoying the music and praise of heaven. It is well with my soul. Lord is there anything more You want to bring about Your grace and truth this morning?'

'No My child. I will give you what you need. What would you like to do now child?'

'Lord You know I love Your Word, and I love going to the Beach.'
Then two things happened simultaneously; I found myself back on the Beach and I knew what I would be searching for: I was to look for gold. As I walked I asked the Lord,
'Will this be a stone of gold Lord or is it the gold setting of the jewels?'
'It is both. You can carry the stone of gold and also know that the settings are of gold. It is the gold of obedience. Now search My Word. Your eyes will be opened. You will love the gold.'

The vision faded, then came another surprise; I knew that I had the gold. It was as swift as that.

---

[231] Psalm 19:1-4 NKJV

Obedience

OBEDIENCE AND GOLD - Gold and Obedience. I wanted to explore the connection between the two. Gold is precious, so is obedience to God. Having been down a gold mine in South Africa, I have learned something of the inordinately lengthy process of extracting gold from rock and the huge ratio of rock to gold. Approximately 4-6grams of gold is extracted from each ton of rock. The value and cost of gold is apparent. A Peruvian gold miner once reported that he needed to extract 30 tons of rock and dirt to recover just one ounce of gold.

And obedience? Is this a long and difficult process too? We find that Jesus, 'Although he was a son, he learned obedience from what he suffered and, once made perfect, he became the source of eternal salvation for all who obey him and was designated by God to be high priest in the order of Melchizedek.'[232]

How did He, the sinless One, learn obedience? Why did He need to? Wasn't He, as the Son Of God already obedient? But He was also Son of Man and open to all the temptations of man. In the previous Chapter 4 of Hebrews, we read that Jesus was tempted with every temptation that man can experience. Yet he was without sin, which is why as our High Priest He can understand our weaknesses. Surely there was an element of

---

[232] Hebrews 5:8-10

suffering involved. He was not exempt from temptation as the Son of Man and had much to overcome. During the hours before His crucifixion, His obedience to the Father was tested to the uttermost - even to the sweating of blood. This was the place of suffering, but He was obedient to the Father, not only in this, but in all the lesser ways of obedience.

HAVE YOU EVER BEEN LOST? WAS HE?

Our first meeting with Jesus in the Bible after His birth illustrates this need for obedience in the young Jesus. He was about twelve at the time. Joseph, Mary and the family had made their annual visit to the Temple in Jerusalem to celebrate the Feast of Passover and they were now on the long journey home with many other families from Nazareth. Unbeknown to them the boy Jesus stayed behind in Jerusalem. Joseph and Mary assumed He was with His friends or other members of the family and did not worry unduly until they looked for Him and discovered He was missing.

After the long walk back to Jerusalem they found Him on the third day in the Temple Courts sitting among the teachers, listening to them and both asking and answering questions. His level of understanding amazed the Jewish religious leaders and when His parents saw Him, they too were amazed.

'His mother said to Him, "Son, Why have you treated us like this? Your father and I have been anxiously searching for you." And He said to them, 'Why were you searching for me? Didn't you know I had to be in my Father's house?"'[233]

At this time, Joseph and Mary did not understand what He was saying. We read that Jesus then went down with them to Nazareth and was subject to them. But His mother kept all these things in her heart.'[234] Jesus knew He was the Son of God and He also knew that his Father's will was that He obey and respect Joseph and Mary.

After this episode we know nothing more until His baptism in the Jordon by John the Baptist. The intervening years were spent in the carpenter's workshop with Joseph. When handling wood day by day, did he ever think of the tree that would eventually be His destiny?

The Temple leaders' amazement was echoed many years later, this time by the common people of Nazareth. They could not understand how He could be so wise and have the power to perform miracles. They had seen Him only as the town carpenter and the eldest in the family of Joseph and Mary. They knew His brothers and His sisters. He had made the townspeople's wooden ploughs, farming implements and furniture. They had passed the time of day with Him and watched him grow up. They asked each other, 'Where did this man get this wisdom and these miraculous powers?'[235] Complaints were voiced. They took offence. Would this have come from jealousy? They were baffled.
Jesus did say that a prophet is never recognised in his own town

---

[233] Luke 2:48b-49
[234] Luke 2:48-51
[235] Matthew 13:54b

and sadly He could not do many miracles there because of their lack of faith. Today there are those who see Him only as a good man.

OBEDIENCE AND FAITH

Faith is often linked with obedience in the Bible. It has been said that obedience without faith is possible but not faith without obedience.

Jesus often required people to act on their faith, and surely He still does. One day when Jesus was in the synagogue He noticed a man with a withered hand. It was a Sabbath,[ii] and both people and Pharisees were watching Him to see if He would heal the man. Mark relates, 'Some of them were looking for a reason to accuse Jesus, so they watched him closely to see if he would heal him on the Sabbath.' The Pharisees were desperate to catch Jesus out on a point of Law and Jesus could read their hearts and their motives. He therefore questioned them on a point of Law, 'Which is lawful on the Sabbath: to do good or to do evil, to save life or to kill?' But they remained silent.'

Jesus looked at them with anger and deep distress. He had already asked the man to stand so that all could see him. Then He asked the man to stretch out his hand.[236] It was a potentially explosive situation and the man could have backed down, but the desire for healing prevailed and in faith he obeyed - and of course was healed by both believing and doing!

---

[236] Mark 3:1-5

Another time, Jesus healed a blind man by putting mud on to his eyes made from the clay on the ground and His own spittle, but the man had to obey Jesus by going to the Siloam pool and washing it off.[iii] This was not an instantaneous healing and presumably he would have had to get someone to lead him to the pool. However, he knew that he must do what Jesus said, once again illustrating obedience and faith.

The most outstanding instance of obedience and faith working together came when Jesus was in the garden of Gethsemane. He was praying to the Father that if it were possible the 'cup' should be removed from Him. This 'cup' involved the Cross and all that it entailed in bearing the sin of mankind, with the inevitable separation from His Father. After much agony which caused Him to sweat drops of blood, His complete obedience won through and He was able to say, 'Yet not what I will but what you will.' [237]

He totally believed that God would not only take Him through the events of the Cross, but also bring Him out into the resurrection. No doubt it was a time when Satan would have taunted and tempted Him to the limit. However, Jesus had many verses of Scripture from the Old Testament in the armoury of His mind which would strengthen His faith. This verse from Psalm 16 written prophetically by David was most apt. 'Therefore my heart is glad and my tongue rejoices; my body also will rest secure, because you will not abandon me to the grave, nor will you let your Holy One see decay.'[238]

---

[237] Mark 14:36b
[238] Psalm 16:9-10

OBEDIENCE, FAITH, AND FREEDOM

There are times when the Word of God comes personally into our dire situations, bringing both comfort and faith for the future. Obedience comes from faith and blessings come from obedience. How these three, faith, obedience and blessings, partner with each other from the Word of God!

In his letter to the Romans, Paul the Apostle reminded the believers that they would be slaves to whomever or whatever they obeyed, the bad or the good. [239] These days we see hundreds if not thousands in obedience to addictions, which rule their lives and lead to illness, poverty, family breakup, mental breakdown and slavery to their habit.

Jesus said to a group of Jews that if they believed and became true disciples, they would know the truth and the truth would make them free. He went on to say, 'So if the Son sets you free you will be free indeed.'[240]

PURE GOLD

Some years ago my husband asked me what I would like for my birthday present. Boldly and hopefully I said if possible I would like a gold watch. Yes it was possible!

I was given a budget allowance and went to our local jeweller to investigate. He gave me three options. What would I like; a watch that looked like gold, a gold plated watch or a solid

---

[239] Romans 6:16
[240] John 8:36

gold watch? This was not a difficult decision! Because he was closing down his business a solid gold Longines watch became mine at a greatly reduced price, just the amount that I had. But that was not the end of it.

As I was driving home some months later, the Lord began to speak. He said that He wanted my life not to just look like gold, nor to be gold plated, but to be solid gold. This was so thought provoking, (and I believe, not just for me.) It would take a lifetime, and amazing grace would be paramount.

HOT, COLD OR LUKEWARM?

The Church in Laodicea thought they were rich and needed nothing. Jesus said that they were neither hot nor cold. Either of those conditions would be better than being lukewarm! He continued, 'I counsel you to buy from Me gold refined in the fire, so that you can become rich.'[241]

Jesus then went on to say that He rebukes and disciplines those He loves. The believers in Laodicea needed to be committed and repent of their lukewarm attitude. Those days of first love, days of delighting in obedience and pleasing their Lord, needed to be revisited. He was looking for that pure gold of love and obedience in the Church, and in this instance, the illustration of refining fire was brought to them.

---

[241] Revelation 3:18

SEND THE FIRE!

Today many Christian songs include words asking God to 'send the fire' and they can easily be sung without full understanding. The 'fire of God' exposes and cleanses sin, bringing holiness. And fire burns! The refiner's fire is very hot and can come in the guise of difficulties, troubles and problems.

We read in the Old Testament of fire falling supernaturally on sacrifices, literally burning them up. Today we are urged to present our bodies as living sacrifices, holy, and pleasing to God, which is our spiritual act of worship.' [242]

We don't like trials and troubles James the Apostle wrote, 'Consider it pure joy, my brothers, whenever you face trials of many kinds, because you know that the testing of your faith develops perseverance.'[243]

Do we likewise desire holiness in our lives? A holiness which not only welcomes but invites the fire to come and burn up all the dross? As we look back, we may realise that God has already sent fire into our lives in many different ways and with differing temperatures. These 'fires' have caused us to seek Him more and to walk in greater loving obedience. As we appreciate more and more His amazing love for us, we understand this in greater depth and maturity.

When we are in his hands we are safe. Then we can look back and know we would not have missed that season of testing for anything. As we have come closer to God we have learned

---

[242] Romans 12:1
[243] James 1:2-3

much. We know for sure that all things do work together for good when we are serving God.[244]

So, gold and obedience - obedience and gold. Both are so precious for the believer because the obedience buys the gold from the Lord, which in eternity causes us to be rich.[245] But what will the Lord ask of us? So we may draw back from Him. Then it is grace which comes to our aid, with love that brings the desire to obey. The battle in our minds is eventually won; the decision made, and with the decision comes peace. Obedience becomes our delight and He is with us in it.

Oswald Chambers writes of the importance of obedience in 'My Utmost for His Highest.' He maintains that it is through the discipline of obedience that we get to the place where Abraham was, that is, seeing who God is. He continues, 'The promises of God are of no value to us until by obedience we understand the nature of God. We read some things in the Bible three hundred and sixty–five times and they mean nothing to us; then all of a sudden we see what God means, because in some particular we have obeyed God, and instantly His nature is opened up.'[246]

Time was passing and I turned once more to the Lord, 'I see that the gold of obedience is the perfect setting for all the precious jewels of Your kingdom Lord.'

This revelation led into more praise and the morning ended.

---

[244] Romans 8:28
[245] Revelation 3:18a
[246] Chambers, O. 1972, p227

O WORSHIP THE LORD IN THE BEAUTY OF HOLINESS,
Bow down before Him, His glory proclaim;
With gold of obedience and incense of lowliness
Kneel and adore him, the Lord is His name.

Low at His feet lay thy burden of carefulness,
High on his heart He will bear it for thee,
Comfort thy sorrows, and answer thy prayerfulness,
Guiding thy steps as may best for thee be.

Fear not to enter His courts in the slenderness
Of the poor wealth though wouldst reckon as thine.
Truth in its beauty, and love in its tenderness,
These are the offerings to lay at His shrine.

These, though we bring them in trembling and fearfulness,
He will accept for the Name that is dear;
Mornings of joy give for evenings of tearfulness,
Trust for our trembling and hope for our fear.

O worship the Lord in the beauty of holiness;
Bow down before Him His glory proclaim;
With gold of obedience and incense of lowliness,
Kneel and adore Him, the Lord is His Name!
John Samuel Bewley Monsell 1863-1875

DAY 13

RIGHTEOUSNESS

'Righteousness exalts a nation; but sin is a reproach to any people,'
Proverbs 14:34
'Blessed are those who hunger and thirst for righteousness, for they shall be filled.' *Matthew 5:6 NKJV*

I AWOKE THIS MORNING with the words, 'It is well with my soul,' on my mind, which led me to the lovely old song of the same name. I read later of the circumstances which led the author to write it. The ship carrying his wife and four daughters to Europe from the United States sank in an accident and only his wife survived. In previous years his son had also died, followed by great financial loss caused by the great Chicago fire of 1871. Through all this sorrow he knew where to look for strength and comfort and could write, 'It is well, it is well with my soul.'

One of the things that I have learned over the years is that when a potential disaster strikes, be it in the area of health, accident, family or finance, the best way to navigate through and remain in peace, is to seek the Lord for His Word on the matter.

When we belong to Him, we have the assurance that He knows and always has known all about it and will take us through in the best possible way. Whatever this involves, the one thing that remains constant is the gift of peace, which is something money cannot buy. We can say with confidence, 'It is well with my soul.'

The Lord and I began to speak,

'These early morning times are so very precious Lord, not to be missed. Thank You for waking me again this morning. What a wonderful and special place to be Lord- in your presence, covered, loved, safe, blessed, happy and joyful, and at peace with You.'

'Are you ready now to move on?'

I was.

'So let us go to the Beach and look and search.'

'Search for what Lord?'

'The stone of My righteousness.'

'Then help me Lord please!'

Wonderful! We were on the Beach once more.

When the Lord said, 'Righteousness,' I had immediately thought of Amos and his vision of the plumb line. The Lord had been showing Amos the prophet that He was going to bring the fire of judgement on Israel, because they were walking in unrighteousness. Amos was pleading with God for mercy, and then he said: 'This is what He showed me.

The Lord was standing by a wall that had been built true to plumb, with a plumb line in His hand. And the Lord asked me, "What do you see, Amos?" "A plumb line," I replied. Then the Lord said, "Look I am setting a plumb line among My people Israel: I will spare them no longer."'[247]

---

[247] Amos 7: 7-8

How many of us have realised the importance of a plumb line when decorating. When I was newly married, my husband and I decided to decorate our bedroom with pale blue and white striped wallpaper. We omitted to use a plumb-line - and the stripes became less vertical at each drop. Enough said. We started again!

'Everything has to be plumb straight' as my father used to say and our heavenly Father says the same to His children.

But now I needed to know more about the stone of righteousness so we began to talk again.

'What am I looking for Lord?'

'This stone is striped. It is a striped stone.'

'Lord, now I am thinking of the stripes that You were given, floggings that left stripes in your body and which brought our healing, and our righteousness. Please teach me about this.'

'So search My Word child.'

With these words in my ears I continued walking across the Beach. Surely a striped stone would be relatively easy to find. There is such beauty in the wet pebbles that I see on this Beach with their many subdued colours and patterns, but the stones that the Lord has been showing me are magnificent, sparkling and full of light. They are precious jewels, not made from stone but created often by supreme pressure.

Suddenly the jewel of righteousness was easy to find. It was conspicuous amongst the pebbles. I picked it up admiring the many colours, stripes blending and swirling together in delightful patterns. It was so beautiful. Then, as so often happened before, my mind began to turn to the Word, and with my eagerness to search its pages, the vision faded.

Righteousness

THE STAR GAZER

A LONG TIME AGO an old man stood looking at the stars and heard God say, 'Now look toward the heavens and count the stars, that is, if you are able to count them.' As the man gazed into the night sky God continued, 'Your offspring will be as numerous as the stars.'[248]

Abraham and his wife Sarah had wanted a child for years but had given up hope. Now, this childless old man, Abraham, believed the Lord. As God spoke, faith to believe this good news was sparked in his heart and mind, and God 'credited it to him as righteousness.'[249]

How can we define 'Righteousness?' At its simplest, it is having or being, in right standing or relationship, before God. This is similar to the place that a child has before its loving parent, or a valued and chosen employee has before his boss - both of them always being confident of being heard, appreciated and accepted.

---

[248] Genesis 15:5
[249] Genesis 15:6

When Abraham heard God speak and believed Him against all the odds, his faith earned him right standing with God.[250] Both he and his wife Sarah were well past the age of producing and bearing a child, yet he continued to believe God for the physically impossible. His faith was to be sorely tested, as the promised son Isaac would not be born for some years after this conversation with God, by which time Abraham was one hundred years old and Sarah his wife was ninety. An even greater testing of his faith came some years later when Isaac was a youth. God spoke again to Abraham and asked him to take this precious son as a sacrifice.

'Then God said, "Take now your son, your only son, Isaac, whom you love, and go to the region of Moriah. Sacrifice him there as a burnt offering on one of the mountains I will tell you about."'[251]

The whole story is a wonderful illustration of both Abraham's obedience and his trust in his God. He was quite sure that the Lord would somehow turn the situation around and he was confident that the two of them would return. So, they set off for Mount Moriah, the mountain that God had indicated, carrying all they needed to build a sacrificial altar.

The Hebrews writer of the New Testament revealed the reason for Abraham's faith, 'Abraham reasoned that God could raise the dead and figuratively speaking, he did receive Isaac back from death.'[252] He knew that God had promised that his

---

[250] Genesis 15:6
[251] Genesis 22:2
[252] Hebrews 11:19

descendants would be as numerous as the stars, so he fully expected God to honour and fulfil His covenant, even if it meant bringing Isaac back from the dead. The Lord of course stopped Abraham from slaying his son at the last moment saying: "Do not lay a hand on the boy, or do anything to him. Now I know that you fear God, because you have not withheld from me your son, your only son."[253]

Then Abraham looked around and saw a ram caught by its horns nearby, which had always been God's intended provision for the sacrifice. [254]

We understand now that this event was a 'shadow' or 'copy,' that prefigured God the Father giving His only Son Jesus as a sacrifice for us. Abraham was shown as a 'type' of God the Father, who was prepared to sacrifice his only son. Isaac was a 'type' of Jesus Christ who was raised from the dead. In the same way, just as Isaac carried the wood on his back on the way to the mountain for the sacrificial fire, so Jesus carried the wood of the Cross on His back to the place of execution.

The ram became the substitute for Isaac just as Jesus Christ was the substitute for us on the Cross, dying for our sins and so providing for us a right standing before God. The ram had also been caught by its horns in a thicket, reminiscent of the crown of thorns that Christ wore on His head. This is an amazing account of God's provision in response to man's obedience

The place of the sacrifice, Mount Moriah, was the place

---

[253] Genesis 22:12
[254] Genesis 22:13

where years later Solomon built the first Temple. Today it is known as the Temple Mount in Jerusalem.

THE MAN OF WOE?

There had been others prior to Abraham, who were righteous in God's sight; for instance, Job, who was a very wealthy and respected man, always looking to please God and lead his grown up family in Godly ways. But now unexpectedly he began to suffer one tragedy after another.

His children were killed, his wealth was taken from him and his good name besmirched. Then his body was attacked and he developed boils from head to foot, so much so that he was only able to sit among the ashes and scrape himself with pieces of pottery. His wife told him to curse God and die but he replied that she was speaking foolishly and wasn't it possible to receive not only good from God but trouble?[255]

Three friends came to comfort him and so great was Job's grief that they sat for seven days without speaking. Then the conversations started. Each one had wonderful things to say but their underlying premise was that this was all Job's fault and God was punishing him because of his sin. However, Job knew that he had a right relationship with God and said so to his friends. They totally rejected this claim and although much of what they said was so good and thought provoking, yet in this one respect they were greatly mistaken.

But God was pleased with Job's replies and his faithful

---

[255] Job 2:9-10

stance. Eventually the severe test that He had allowed came to an end and God poured blessings upon him. His losses were more than restored, so that he ended with double the number of livestock previously owned. He fathered a new family, seven sons and three daughters who were considered the most beautiful in all the land and he was blessed to see his sons and grandsons to four generations.

The turning point in the story came when the Lord spoke to both Job and his friends. They were to ask Job to pray for them, as they had been in the wrong, and this prayer would bring forgiveness. Job also repented knowing that he had spoken in ignorance.

How and why had this severe time in Job's life come about? Job was unaware that Satan had approached God; taunting Him that Job was only obedient because God had so blessed him with riches and goods. In effect, Satan was saying, 'Just let me get at Job and then we will see a different story.' But God trusted Job's integrity and allowed Satan to test him within limits; his life was to be sacrosanct. In all this, Job remained faithful.

There are times when we, like Job, ask ourselves, 'Why is this happening?' and God may or may not give us His reasons. When we know the Lord, as Job did, we can rest assured that our God is trustworthy, faithful, and will not let us go.

Noah was another such man. It is said that he found favour in the eyes of the Lord. He was a righteous man and

blameless in his time, and he walked with God.[256]
The earth's population at this time was increasing in number and, 'The Lord saw how great man's wickedness on the earth had become, and that every inclination of the thoughts of his heart was only evil all the time. The Lord was grieved that he had made man on the earth, and his heart was filled with pain.'[257] God therefore decided to send the great flood, preserving only this blameless man Noah and his family, with a variety of animals. Jesus verified this much loved story in Matthew's Gospel,[258] as did the prophet Isaiah, the Apostle Peter and the writer to the Hebrews.

KNOW YOUR ANCESTORS?

Today many people are getting interested in genealogy and finding some surprises in their ancestry. Christ's genealogy also holds some surprises.[259] Far from being rather uninteresting parts of scripture, we discover that a genealogy can contain a wealth of knowledge and interest. Again we see Noah amongst the names.[260] He had the faith that would sustain him through a hundred years of building a specialist ship, the Ark, amidst the scorn and derision of passersby. After all they would say, 'who needs a ship on dry land?' So again, faith was linked with righteousness and also with action.

---

[256] Genesis 6:9b
[257] Genesis 6:5-6
[258] Matthew 24:37-39
[259] Matthew1 and Luke 3
[260] Luke 3:36

Rahab lived many generations later. She was the prostitute who gave shelter to the two spies that Joshua sent to spy out Jericho and the land. When the king of Jericho heard of this, he insisted that Rahab turn these men in, and sent officials to get them. However, she was beginning to be convinced that the Israelites had a valid mission, so she hid them under stalks of flax on the roof and told the King's officials that they had already left. Afterwards she spoke to the spies and asked for safety for herself and her family, acknowledging that the 'Lord your God; He is God in heaven above and on earth beneath.'[261] She and her family were accepted into the Israelite family and she married a man called Salmon and through him her family tree became famous in Jewish history. Rahab's first son Boaz, became the great-grandfather of King David.[262]

Further down the line, David became the ancestor of Mary's husband Joseph. So too Rahab, the woman of sin, in acknowledging God, was included in Christ's genealogy. It is also interesting that she let the spies down from her house on the wall, by a scarlet cord. She was later instructed to bind the scarlet cord round the window to identify her property when the fighting started. This red line was her salvation from death, reminding us of the blood of Christ, our salvation.

---

[261] Joshua 2:11b
[262] Matthew1:5-6

EXCHANGE IS NO ROBBERY

How many times have we as children 'swapped' toys with friends, 'for keeps,' always confident that we were getting the better deal. In a similar way God has given to us His righteousness. Derek Prince explained it in terms of a 'Divine Exchange,' taking the concept from 2 Corinthians. 'God made Him who had no sin to be sin for us, so that in him we might become the righteousness of God.'[263]

However, this exchange is one which is fully initiated and put into practice by God Himself. Christ who was sinless took our sin upon Himself on the Cross and in exchange gave us His righteousness. Good News indeed

PROTECTION - BEHAVIOUR -REWARDS -BESSINGS

- PART OF the Christian's **protection** in spiritual warfare is the breastplate of righteousness.[264] The firm knowledge of one's righteousness before God provides help against condemnation, which Satan will try to put on us at every opportunity.
- THERE ARE many descriptions of righteous **behavior** in the Bible. We are reminded that there should not even be a hint of sexual immorality or greed among God's people. Care should also be taken with speech so that there is no foolish talk, obscenity or coarse jokes. It is better to be giving thanks for blessings. '[265]

---

[263] 2 Corinthians 5:21
[264] Ephesians 6:14b
[265] Ephesians 5:4

- THERE ARE **rewards** for holy living. The Lord says that He is coming quickly and He is bringing His reward to every one according to what he has done.[266]
- THERE ARE many **blessings** for the righteous like this promise in 1Peter 3:12 (NKJV)
'For the eyes of the Lord are on the righteous, and his ears are open to their prayers.'

However, time was moving on and I turned to prayer, relieved and thankful that when God looks at me, He sees His Son's righteousness on me.

Then He spoke again echoing my thoughts,

'My righteousness child. For you. Through Jesus Christ.'

'Amen Lord.'

My morning came to a close.

---

[266] Revelation 22:12

WHEN PEACE LIKE A RIVER, ATTENDETH MY WAY,
When sorrows like sea billows roll,
Whatever my lot, thou hast taught me to say
It is well; it is well with my soul.

Though Satan should buffet, though trials come,
Let this blest assurance control,
That Christ has regarded my helpless estate,
And hath shed His own blood for my soul.

My sin, oh the bliss of this glorious thought!
My sin, not in part but the whole,
Is nailed to the Cross, and I bear it no more,
Praise the Lord, praise the Lord, O my soul.

And Lord, haste the day when the faith shall be sight,
The clouds be rolled back as a scroll.
The trumpet shall sound and the Lord shall descend,
Even so, it is well with my soul.

Horatio Spafford 1828-1888

Death

DAY 14

DEATH

"Be faithful even to the point of death, and I will give you the crown of life.'   *Revelation 2:10b* NKJV

ONCE MORE A NEW MORNING, and I am anticipating time with the Lord on the Beach. Which jewel will I be looking for today? In the event, it was to be the most unusual of all the mornings and to start with the most difficult. After a wonderful time of worship, I was quickly on the Beach and straight away could see in my mind's eye a most glorious purple jewel.
Then the Lord spoke;
'Look for the beautiful large purple stone that I have just shown you. Its beauty is sending out lovely light. You will have to search for it My child.'

Just hearing the Lord speak causes me to praise Him as I walk along, and I ask Him to lead me to this extraordinarily beautiful and precious stone. But what is its name and what does it mean? Even as I was asking Him, the revelation came and I knew what it was. This lovely stone was 'Death' and I stopped. What did the Lord want to show me?

'Yes My child, but don't be alarmed. When you find it and search its meaning you will rejoice with Me and we will dance and rejoice together. So don't fear this stone this morning.

Remember its deep, deep beauty - how lovely it looks - beautiful facets in the light. Are you willing?'

I was willing, knowing I must trust Him and put aside my hesitant thoughts. I carried on walking and looking. After a while something happened. I could feel the stone in my hand. The search was over and I began to examine this beautiful jewel, turning it this way and that. It was so lovely that I wanted to spend some time looking at it and absorbing its calm and deep purple beauty.

After a while I knew that I also needed to know His Word on this. At the same time the chorus of a hymn written by Helen Lemmel came to mind which was a comfort,
'Turn your eyes upon Jesus. Look full in His wonderful face
And the things of earth will grow strangely dim,
In the light of His glory and grace.'

As I continued to look, I realised that the stone was set into a ring.

'Yes child. This ring is an adornment for you. You can look at it on your finger - or you can hold it in your hand and look at it. I give it to you as an adornment to wear. Will you?'
Yes, I knew I would wear it and I put it on the finger of my right hand, praising the Lord for such wonderful jewels that He was giving me.

'These are kingdom gifts My child, signs and aspects of truths of My kingdom - adornments.'
I needed to look into the Word. Why Death this morning? What was the Lord trying to show me?

Death

IT SEEMED GOOD to visit the book of Genesis once more. There, the newly created Adam walked and talked with his Creator, in the most beautiful of all gardens - trees, flowers, fruits, birds, animals, peace and loveliness. Interestingly, the first conversation between them that we know of in this Paradise was about death.

Two very special trees were in the centre of the garden - the Tree of Life and the Tree of the Knowledge of Good and Evil. We don't know when the following conversation took place but surely it would have been soon after Adam's creation. The Lord told Adam that he could eat from any of the trees in the garden apart from one. A severe warning followed: the Lord God emphasised that although he could freely eat from the trees in the garden, eating from the Tree of the Knowledge of Good and Evil would surely cause him to die on that day.[267]

Had Adam seen death in this sinless and blessed garden of perfection? We do not know, but Adam would have realised that God was issuing a severe warning. Thus far, he had not been denied anything. Yet later, when Eve started to eat from the tree, and offered him one of the forbidden fruits, he ate. Death came in more than one way. The immediate result was

---

[267] Genesis 2:16-17

spiritual death, that is, the death of their spirits, the part of them that was the communication centre with God. Now that his spirit was dead, his soul took over the dominant role; the soul being the seat of the mind, the will and the emotions.

Chuck Smith puts it like this,

'With man's spirit uppermost, there was a beautiful communion and fellowship with God. But when man obeyed the body appetites, eating of this tree, man became inverted and he became body, soul and spirit. The spirit now out of touch with God is dead. It has lost the awareness and consciousness of God. It's lying here dormant and the uppermost thing that now rules the mind of man is the body and the body needs. The desires of the flesh now rule over man.'[268] This would be overturned at the Cross centuries later.

In the book of Ephesians Chapter 2, the Apostle Paul explains how this spiritual death was reversed by Christ. He says that we were dead in trespasses and sins and by nature children of wrath. But because of God's rich mercy and love, He made us alive together with Christ, when we were saved by grace. This is why we need to be born again, born of the Spirit, as Jesus told Nicodemus. Once our spirit is alive to God, we can hear him, desire obedience to Him, and enjoy wonderful, loving fellowship with Him. Paul commented on this, saying, 'Therefore, if anyone is in Christ, he is a new creation; the old has gone, the new has come!'[269]

---

[268] Smith, Chap. 3 Sermon on Genesis
[269] 2 Corinthians 5:17

Results of the Disobedience
- Fear came upon Adam and Eve and they tried to hide from the presence of God.
- Spiritual death came.
- They were banished from the Garden.
- Curses came upon the earth.
- Physical death was introduced for all mankind.
- The sin nature became manifest in all.

Obeying Satan had given him power and authority on earth. How was God going to bring restoration to that which was lost in the garden? The only One who could break Satan's domination was God's Son Jesus Christ. This He did at the Cross by taking the sin of mankind upon himself by His sacrificial death.

The Holy Spirit through the Apostle Paul teaches us that God had further expectations regarding this sacrifice, 'And he died for all, that those who live should no longer live for themselves but for him who died for them and was raised again.'[270] God was looking for a saved people who would be His special people. This special people would live for God rather than themselves. Restoration and reconciliation between man and God thereby opened the way for man to regain spiritual communication and fellowship with God.
Death came in with the first Adam - life came with Jesus Christ, the 'second Adam.'[271]

---

[270] 2 Corinthians 5:15
[271] 1Corinthians 15:45

The Adamic sin nature now dominant in man was reflected in the Old Testament history of God's chosen people Israel. Sin and death curl their way through all the pages, yet woven through these long years are the promises that God sent by his prophets. A time would come when the Messiah would bring salvation, a time when the Lord would pour His mercy on mankind and destroy death forever.

'On this mountain The Lord of Hosts will prepare a feast of rich food for all peoples, a banquet of aged wine – the best of meats, and the finest of wines. On this mountain He will destroy the shroud that enfolds peoples, the sheet that covers all nations; he will swallow up death forever. The Sovereign Lord God will wipe away the tears from all faces; he will remove disgrace from his people from all the earth. The Lord has spoken.'[272]

This is a foretelling of the time when Jesus Christ comes to the earth again to rule and reign. God's immense patience with and compassion for His people, Jew and Gentile, will be demonstrated.

RICH MAN POOR MAN

Jesus told a story of two men who died, one was rich and lacked nothing and one a beggar, Lazarus, lacked everything.
The rich man died and went to Hades and eternal suffering, and the poor man to Abraham's Bosom, the place of eternal blessing. But for a few words at the end of the story we might

---

[272] Isaiah 25:6-8

think that Jesus inferred that the rich go the hell and the poor go to heaven. However the rich man in Hades was pleading for his brothers to have a chance to repent and be saved from this eternal suffering. If Abraham could only send Lazarus back to earth he could warn his five brothers! They would surely repent if someone went back from the dead to tell them what the future held. Abraham replied that if they did not listen to Moses and the prophets they would not be persuaded even if one rose from the dead. So the issue was that of a repentant life before God.

It is thought that Jesus may have been recounting a real situation, as this is the only story He told where personal names are used. Even so, Lazarus the naturally poor man was the spiritually rich man. He was the one who had enjoyed a relationship with God.

THE 23RD PSALM

'Even though I walk through the valley of the shadow of death, I will fear no evil; for you are with me; your rod and your staff, they comfort me.'[273]

Here David is talking about death. He has the confidence and faith in God to be able to speak of the valley, not of death, but of the *shadow* of death. Shadows cannot harm us, and there is no need for the believer to be frightened. He saw it as a walk through a valley, with the Lord God showing the way, as a shepherd would lead his sheep.

---

[273] Psalm 23:4

IS IT EVER TOO LATE?

The two criminals with Jesus on Roman crosses were facing imminent and inevitable death. Both would enter eternity yet to opposite destinations, dependent upon on their attitude to Jesus. Only to the believing thief on the cross next to Him, did Jesus promise life in Paradise that day.[274] For the other thief, it would be too late.

He gave this comfort and promise to His disciples on the eve of His crucifixion, 'Do not let your hearts be troubled. You believe in God; believe also in Me. In My Father's house are many rooms; if it were not so would I would have told you that I am going there to prepare a place for you? And if I go and prepare a place for you, I will come back and take you to be with me that you also may be where I am.'[275]
A firm promise of comfort for the faithful believer.

Some believe that death means the total end of man's existence; a seamless exit from life into blackness and 'nothingness'. This would mean no judgement and therefore the freedom to live life according to one's whims. They have not understood that there is more to man than his body and it is only the body that dies. The soul goes on into eternity. God has set eternity into the heart of man.[276]
The death that the Lord warns about is not annihilation, but the prospect of being eternally separated from God and of eternal

---

[274] Luke 23:43
[275] John 14:1-3
[276] Ecclesiastes 3:11b

punishment.[277]

The culmination of blessing for the believer comes when the Lord returns again and is given a new glorious body in which to live out eternity.[278] In older age, the thought of having a new body like the resurrection body of Jesus becomes increasingly attractive. When we know the wonderful promises that are there for us, they become as facets of the beautiful purple jewel and the fear of death diminishes.

AND AFTERWARDS?

Looking far into the future, there is to be a new heaven and a new earth where the New Jerusalem will be situated. There will be no more tears as God will wipe them away. Death will no longer exist, neither grief nor crying nor pain. All of that will have passed away.[279]

As we continue to read in the book of Revelation we find descriptions of The New Jerusalem, the foundation walls of which are jewels and each gate a single pearl. The street is pure gold and a sparkling river runs alongside, with the tree of life there for all. There is no darkness and no curse in this place.[280]

All this and more is the future for those who have trusted God's Son and followed His ways. This is why the purple jewel is so glorious.

---

[277] Matthew 25:31-46
[278] Philippians 3:21
[279] Revelation 21:4
[280] Revelation 21 and 22

Then the Lord spoke the final word as the morning came to a close to which I could only say, 'Amen.'

'Now you see why this stone is so beautiful.'

Oswald Chambers

Oswald Chambers may not be a familiar name to many today, but his daily writings in 'My Utmost for His Highest' have been, and are, prized by countless Christians. They are taken from lectures given by him at the Bible Training College, Clapham from 1911 to 1915, and afterwards from talks given in Egypt until 1917, the year of his death.

August 5th My Utmost for His Highest

The Baffling Call of God

And all things that are written by the prophets concerning the Son of man shall be accomplished...And they understood none of these things. Luke 18:31, 34

God called Jesus Christ to what seemed unmitigated disaster. Jesus Christ called His disciples to see Him put to death; he led every one of them to the place where their hearts were broken. Jesus Christ's life was an absolute failure from every standpoint but God's. But what seemed failure from man's standpoint was tremendous triumph from God's, because God's purpose is never man's purpose.

There comes the baffling call of God in our lives also. The call of God can never be stated explicitly; it is implicit. The call of God is like the call of the sea; no-one hears it but the one who has the call of the sea in him. It cannot be stated definitely what the call of God is to, because His call is to be in comradeship with Himself for His own purpose, and the test is to believe that God knows what He is after. The things that happen do not happen by chance, they happen entirely in the decree of God. God is working out His purposes.

If we are in communion with God and recognise He is taking us into His purposes, we shall no longer try to find out what His purposes are. As we go on in the Christian life it gets simpler, because we are less inclined to say - 'Now why did God allow this and that?' Behind the whole thing lies the compelling of God. 'There's a divinity that shapes our ends.' A Christian is one who trusts the wits and wisdom of God, and not his own wits. If we have a purpose of our own, it destroys the simplicity and the leisureliness which ought to characterize the children of God.[281]

---

[281] Chambers, 1972, p153

Treasure

DAY 15

TREASURE!

'For where your treasure is, there will your heart be also.' *Matthew 6:21*

'Then the Almighty himself will be your treasure. He will be your gold and precious silver!' *Job 22:25 NLT*

LATER THAT DAY, after the earlier revelations about the purple jewel of death, I went to a Church day conference, and there something unusual happened. I found myself unexpectedly taken in vision to the Beach again during the worship time. This was a surprise as it was during the daytime and in the company of many other believers.

I was on the Beach. As I looked ahead I saw that it was covered with precious stones. The sand and pebbles could not be seen for the colours of the myriads of jewels. Then I saw little hillocks of jewels piled high, getting bigger and bigger; they were precious stones of the kingdom. Such richness! There were more than enough for all believers.
Then I realised that I had the grace stone in my hand. I was holding it in my right hand, on which was the lovely purple jewel. I began to understand that all the stones, the precious jewels that I had seen and the ones still to come are available to

all, through the grace of God and through death of Christ.

The vision changed. I was before a throne. Jesus was there in His glory - standing in front of the throne. The path leading to the throne was made up of all the precious jewels. Treasure! He was walking on them.

This picture was over in a flash and I was back on the Beach. Then the Lord spoke and said;

'The Beach is a public Beach child, not a private one. All may walk on this Beach and see the stones as you have done. You may share it as I lead you My child. Hear My voice in this.'

As I looked again at the Beach I saw crowds of people. 'I see lots of people walking on the Beach now Lord. Do they know what they are looking for or why are they there? Will you tell them?'

'I will tell them and you can share too. You seem to know child, don't you that the walk on the Beach starts when you have spent time with Me in praise and worship.'

'Yes!'

Then the vision faded. Public worship continued.

Thoughts

© 'Thoughts' 2015 Joy Sands

Lord, help me hear your very whisper.
Let not my guileful heart be so cold
That I think only of the world
And the clamour of it, drowning
The quiet gentle insistence of Your voice.

Lord, help me walk the steady way of wisdom.
Carefully place my feet where You would go;
The narrow path is hard to bear.
And those I love would take the other road
That seems to beckon, wide and clear,
But, leading where?
O My dear child, have a care.

Lord, help me see with eyes that understand;
That look with love and cause kind words to soothe.
Not letting thoughts of selfish pride
Open gates that hurt, deride and move
My heart away from all that murmurs 'Peace.'
No, let your oil so warm flow gently down
To heal the troubled soul.

Lord help me speak with words that bring Your love,
Which causes those who turn away
To pause and hear the words not said,
Yet making hearts to weep and break with sorrow.
Gentle Breeze, breathe softly hardened walls,
Releasing fear and images so aged and old,
Still creeping, touching, spoiling.

Lord, let me not be seen,
Instead may You appear,
You who are my very life,
And in my thoughts both day and night.
Holy Breath so sweet to comfort,
Check the tears, and open wide the arms that call 'Come home!
For all is peace, the price is paid.
Just look My child, my hands, my feet, my side.'

Crowns

DAY 16

CROWNS

'Crown him with many crowns the Lamb upon His throne.'
Matthew Bridges 1852
'No pain, no palm; no thorns, no throne; no gall, no glory; no cross, no crown'   *W. Penn founder of Pennsylvania. 1669*

A NEW DAY! After the morning with the lovely purple death jewel and then the short vision at the conference, I was a little hesitant, wondering what else the Lord would show me. As always, praise and worship draw me back to Him. And then,
'Are You prepared for a surprise this morning My child?'
'Yes Lord. Your surprises are always good ones.'
And the Holy Spirit took me back into praise for some time.
    Then once more, I was quickly on the Beach. Everywhere looked glorious, warm, sunny and clear. This Beach is such a wonderful place to be, the sound of gentle waves, sunshine, peace. I kept walking and as I was enjoying the scene, I saw something new.
'Lord I think there's a rainbow over the Beach today. There is light coming from it and all its colours are dancing on the pebbles.'
(I also know that there are angels dancing in the air.)
The rainbow is always the sign of My covenant promise My

child.'

As the Lord is speaking I see something just ahead and walk towards it, but it is not another jewel. It looks like a parcel of some sort.

'I see a package today Lord. Is this the surprise, not a jewel but a parcel?'

'Yes child. A package this morning for you to unwrap. A gift.'

And then came the biggest surprise of all - I opened it and found it was a crown. I was stunned!

'You can wear it this morning. A crown of beauty for you.'

I was overwhelmed and as we continued to talk, the Lord was assuring me that the crown was for me, but it was too much for me to take in. He was calling it a crown of faithfulness and righteousness, but how could any of this be ours, apart from His presence and grace in our lives? How can He give us crowns when we should be giving Him crowns?

And then I remembered the rainbow that I had seen earlier and asked the Lord about it.

'When I saw the rainbow I thought that today would be about Covenant, Lord.'

But He did not answer except to direct my thoughts back to crowns,

'And I have this crown for you. Righteousness.'

But still I was protesting.

'No. It is Your righteousness Lord. Nothing of me.'

'Would you like to research crowns My child. You will enjoy it and be surprised.'

It sounded like a lovely adventure to me. Then I realised there was something else,

'Lord I sense there is perfume here. I can't smell it, but I know it's here. It is your presence Lord.'

He replied,

'Remember the perfume of Mary. An eternal reality.'

At this point, for some reason I was worried about deception and asked the Lord about it. So we talked and my prayer was; 'Lord please sharpen my discernment in these days, as deception is so subtle.'

And He said,

'There will always be a perfume of loveliness about My presence and My Word. The enemy has no access to this lovely perfume. Also there is My peace in your heart and joy with it. The enemy has no access to peace or joy, that deep joy in your heart. And My Word, it is your plumb line in all matters, My truth.'

'Lord help me to keep aware and awake at all times; wisdom Lord too.'

'Keep looking to Me. I provide all you need.'

It was then time to look into 'crowns' in His Word.

Crowns

CROWNS HAVE ALWAYS BEEN a sign of power, authority, and honour. Rulers' crowns have often mirrored their owners' wealth an importance, gold and precious gems telling their own story. Simple but highly prized crowns of wreaths were given to celebrate victory in sport in ancient Rome and Greece. A different type of crown altogether is one that a husband may wear, but it depends on his wife. The Word says that if she is an excellent wife then she herself is his crown.[282] Looking at a few verses further on, grey hair is spoken of as a crown of glory and found in the way of righteousness.

Isaiah, speaking by the power of the Holy Spirit said that the Lord will be like a beautiful crown and a glorious diadem to the remnant of Israel 'in that day.' What a wonderful promise for Israel– 'that day' speaking of God's total deliverance of Israel in end times. [283]

However, when we look into the New Testament, we find that just as kings are given crowns, so the Lord has crowns for us
The Apostles further tell us who will wear these crowns.

---

[282] Proverbs 12:4
[283] Isaiah 28:5

The eternal crown is for those who are faithful:

Comparing the Christian life to a race, Paul writes something that is relevant in today's Olympic Games; 'Do you not know that in a race all the runners run, but only one gets the prize? Run in such a way as to get the prize. Everyone who competes in the games goes into strict training. They strive to get a crown that will fade; but our crown that will last forever.'[284]
This crown is for the follower of Christ who remains faithful to the end.

The crown of righteousness, for those who eagerly look forward to his return:

The Apostle Paul also says of himself and others; 'I have fought the good fight, I have finished the race, I have kept the faith. Now there is in store for me the crown of righteousness, which the Lord, the righteous Judge will award to me on that day, and not only to me, but also to all who have longed for His appearing.'[285]

This letter to Timothy was probably Paul's last letter, as he knew that his martyrdom was imminent. Not long afterwards he was beheaded in Rome, a quick death as he was a Roman citizen. Not so for the Apostle Peter, who according to tradition was crucified upside down by choice; he did not consider himself worthy to suffer the same way as his Saviour.

---

[284] 1 Corinthians 9:24-25
[285] 2 Timothy 4:7-8

This was a much changed man from the one who had boasted much and then denied His Lord.

The crown of righteousness is for the faithful believer who looks forward with delight to the Lord's appearing at His second coming. He is confident in his relationship with Him and anticipates with assurance eternity spent with Him.

The crown of life for those who endure:

James, who always referred to himself as the slave of God and Jesus Christ, said that the man who endures under trials and temptations shall receive the crown of life, a promise from the Lord to all who love Him.[286]

We see one of the ways that the believer would be tried and tested in the letter to the Church in Smyrna. In it, Jesus Christ gave the believers both insight into future troubles and the promise of the crown of life for those who remained faithful.

'Do not be afraid of what you are about to suffer. I tell you, the devil will put some of you in prison, to test you, and you will suffer persecution for ten days. Be faithful even to the point of death, and I will give you the crown of life.'[287]

We know that in the 20th Century, millions of Christians have already walked this road. It continues unabated in this new century as we draw nearer to the time of Christ's return.

---

[286] James 1:12
[287] Revelation 2:10

The unfading crown of glory for faithful elders:
There is the special crown for those church leaders who have been faithful servants to their flock.

Peter teaches about the qualifications for the elders of the churches, and the crown that they will receive.
'To the elders among you, I appeal as a fellow elder, a witness of Christ's sufferings and one who will also share in the glory to be revealed; be shepherds of God's flock that is under your care, not because you must, but because you are willing, as God wants you to be; not greedy for money, but eager to serve; not lording it over those entrusted to you, but being examples to the flock. And when the Chief Shepherd appears, you will receive the crown of glory that will never fade away.'[288] What a blessing such church leaders are to their flock.

We might think that these crowns are guaranteed to all Christians, but there is a sober warning by Jesus to the Philadelphian Church. This was the only Church not to have specific problems mentioned, but they were told to hold fast to what they had, so that no-one would take their crown. What was Jesus talking about? What was the warning? It was the possibility of losing their crown.
'I am coming soon! Hold on to what you have, so that no one will take your crown.'[289]
In other words Jesus was saying, 'keep on keeping on! Don't lose what you have - hold fast!'

Jesus Himself walked the way of suffering and wore the

---

[288] 1Peter 5:1- 4
[289] Revelation 3:11

crown that was in the world's eyes a sign of mockery. Just prior to His crucifixion, Jesus was scourged with whips by the Roman soldiers, then stripped and clothed with a scarlet robe. To complete the picture of 'kingship' they twisted together a crown of thorns, put it on His head and put a stick in His hand. Then came the mockery, spitting and scorn as they knelt down saying, 'Hail King of the Jews'. [290] They beat His head with the stick, driving in the thorns. How many of these soldiers would have repented with tears in time to come?

It is good to be able to write on this Easter Sunday that now the risen and glorified Jesus Christ wears the crown of glory and honour[291] and one day we will see Him. We will surely place any crowns we have been given at Jesus' feet, knowing that we have only received them by His grace.

We read in Revelation of the honours that come to us. 'He has made us to be kings and priests to God,' or by another translation, He has made us 'a kingdom of priests to God.' Furthermore, we shall reign on the earth. To whom is the Apostle John referring? [292] Surely he is speaking of all those who have become Christians – followers of Jesus Christ – purchased by His blood.

---

[290] Matthew 27:28-30
[291] Hebrews 2:9
[292] Revelation 5:9-10

The Starry Crown

There is yet another crown worn by the woman in the book of Revelation who was introduced as a 'sign' in heaven. She was clothed with the sun, with the moon under her feet, and she wore a crown of twelve stars.[293] What a magnificent crown! There are various interpretations of who she is. As she gave birth to a son who is to rule the nations with a rod of iron' (which would refer to Jesus Christ), she could be Mary. But more likely she could be the picture of Israel.

We know that Scripture confirms Scripture and back in the Old Testament Joseph had dreamed that the sun and the moon and eleven stars bowed down to him.[294] When he shared this with his family, his father Jacob rebuked him and asked him what sort of a dream did he think he had; did he expect that he and his mother and brothers would one day bow down to him? This dream certainly caused friction, but of course it is exactly what happened.

It became a reality when years later Joseph became the second ruler in Egypt. His father, mother and ten of his brothers came to him pleading for food to alleviate the famine they were experiencing in Canaan. They did not recognize Joseph and in the presence of this mighty ruler in Egypt, they were required to bow down.

There may be other interpretations regarding this scripture - nevertheless, what a glorious crown!

---

[293] Revelation 12:1
[294] Genesis 37:9-10

Finally

In Revelation 19 we find a description of the risen and glorified Jesus, the King of Kings and the Lord of Lords. He is shown on a white horse, His eyes like a flame of fire and wearing many crowns. He is about to return to earth and is ready for war against His enemies on the earth. Victory is imminent.

His second advent will be very different from His first. Then He came as the world's Saviour, humbly born in a stable, the Lamb of God and the sacrifice for sin. Now, He comes as conqueror, to set up His righteous millennial kingdom on earth and every knee will bow and every eye will see His coming.[295]

After this study I was able to speak with the Lord again. 'This has been another wonderful morning Lord. I give You my crown, worn for a short time with You. I cast it to your feet and thank you for a very special time today. Indeed, it was such a surprise.'
The Lord then asked me what I had learned about crowns. I realised that one of the most important things is the promise of crowns waiting for all the faithful disciples of Jesus Christ.

'I'm glad you're pleased child. We have had a lovely time together.'
'Yes Lord. Indeed.'
So, after many nights of exploring the Beach with the Lord and gathering precious jewels, this extraordinary month came to an end. It has been one of the most amazing months I have ever experienced with Him. The visions were mostly spent on the Beach; but not all, as there were other places and other visions, but maybe these are for another time.

---

[295] Revelation 1:7

POST SCRIPT

During the writing of this, I heard that it is often hard to finish a book; there always seems to be more. This is so! When describing the truths of these jewels, how is it possible to put the final full stop on a topic like grace, or love, which has not three but four dimensions; the breadth, length, height and depth?[296] Or how can we fully describe the Kingdom, which in experience and revelation is unending?

So indeed this book, taken from my journal, is by definition, a series of cameos or tasters.

A journal touches on just a little, and as we believers walk through life, we learn and experience more and more. We are constantly discovering that what we thought we knew and understood is but a fraction of the reality, and the more we know, the more we realise how little we know.

I am reminded of Ezekiel's prophecy where he was walking through the river that flowed from the Temple. At first the water was ankle deep, then gradually it rose to waist height, and then it became so deep that his feet no longer touched the bottom and he had to swim. So it is with us and our walk with God.

However, I trust that you have enjoyed these times on the Beach. As you develop a real hunger and thirst for the Lord and His Word, then according to His Word you will be satisfied.[297]

---

[296] Ephesians 3:18
[297] Psalm 17: 15 and Matthew 5:6

[1]i) p 191. Interestingly, since writing this I have discovered that according to Dwight A. Pryor, who was a founding board member of the Jerusalem School of Synoptic Research in Israel and Founder/President of the Center for Judaic-Christian Studies, in Dayton, Ohio, 'extensive research has shown that in fact healing on the Sabbath was allowed and not considered work I am indebted to Tim Ayers for this information, taken from Mr Pryor's CD 'Our Hebrew Lord'. Tape 4

ii) p 191 'Again the duplicity and antagonism of the Sadducees and scribes against Jesus is obvious. For example:
Jesus' action of putting spittle into the blind man's eyes; Jewish tradition taught that the oldest son had healing properties in his saliva. So here again Jesus uses their tradition to show that He indeed had power to heal.' (T. Ayers)

Bibliography

BRIDGES, G. (2006 2nd.Ed.) *The Discipline Of Grace.* Colorado Springs: NAVPRESS.

CHAMBERS, O. (1972) *My Utmost For His Highest.* 2nd Ed
London: Oswald Chambers Publications Association. Marshall, Morgan & Scott.

CHAMBERS, O (1989) *The Place of Help.* Grand Rapids: Oswald Chambers Association Limited

DEAN-DELIU, F. (2011) *Embarking on an Intimate Journey with the Holy Spirit.* Pittsburg: Dorrance Publishing Co.

DOYLE, T. (2012) *Dreams and Visions.* Nashville: Thomas Nelson Inc.

GRAHAM, B. (1984) *Peace With God.* Nashville: Thomas Nelson Inc.

GRUBB, N P (1952) *Rees Howells, Intercessor:* Cambridge: The Lutterworth Press

LENNOX, J (2015) *Against The Flow.* Oxford UK: Monarch Books

Color Magazine International Colored Gem Association.

MAIER, P. (1999) *Eusebius The Church History. A New Translation with Commentary.*
Grand Rapids: Kregal Publications

TEN BOOM, C. SHERRILL, J & E (1971) *The Hiding Place.* Grand Rapids: Chosen Books.

RUSSELL, K. (CHAPLAIN) (2014) Sermon delivered at St. David's Cathedral at The Annual National Battle of Britain Commemoration. 2014Hobart

RYLE, J. (1970) *One Blood, The UpperRoom.* Carlisle: Banner of Truth.

SMITH, C. *2000 Study guides series on Genesis 2-3:* Rancho Santa Margarita: Blue Letter Bible

THE UNKNOWN CHRISTIAN. (1986) *The Kneeling Christian.* Grand Rapids: Zondervan

Crowns